girlfriends
get together

girlfriends
get together

Food, Frolic and Fun Times!

Carmen Renee Berry, Tamara Traeder,
and Janet Hazen

Wildcat Canyon Press
A Division of Circulus Publishing Group, Inc.
Berkeley, California

girlfriends get together: Food, Frolic, and Fun Times!

Editorial Director: Roy M. Carlisle
Managing Editor: Leyza Yardley
Marketing Director: Carol Brown
Production Coordinator: Larissa Berry
Copyeditor: Virginia Alderson Hoffman
Proofreader: Susan Hindman
Cover Photo: Hulton-Getty Images/Stone
Cover Design: Mary Beth Salmon
Illustrations: Mike Powell
Interior Design and Typesetting: Saffron Creative
Typographic Specifications: Body text set in Cochin 11/15 and Frutiger Light Condensed 11/16. Headers set in Copperplate 32 17/14.4, Muriel 35/25 and Kaufmann 27/25.

Printed in Canada

Library of Congress Cataloging-in-Publication Data
Berry, Carmen Renee.
   girlfriends get together : food, frolic, and fun times / Carmen Renee Berry, Tamara
Traeder, and Janet Hazen.
      p. cm.
   Includes index.
   ISBN 1-885171-53-6 (alk. paper)
   1. Cookery. 2. Entertaining. 3. Female Friendship. I. Traeder, Tamara, 1960- II. Hazen,
Janet. III. Title.

TX714 .B3956 2001
642'.4--dc21
                                                                        00-069313

Distributed to the trade by Publishers Group West
10 9 8 7 6 5 4 3 2 1

The Girlfriends Creed

We will know each other in our lifetimes. We will not be secrets from each other.

We will say what we want to say now and not wait until a passing.

Our friendships are living, tangible realities, in which we rejoice.

May we always come together when we are able.

May we always give our stories freely and have space in which to hear them.

May we always get dressed up — every once in a while in our fashion —

Give our best and widest grin,

And raise our teacups high.

—*KC Chapek*

Contents

Gather All Girlfriends!

Think back—when were the times you have felt a sense of belonging, had the most fun or experienced the greatest comfort? Chances are many of those moments were spent with your girlfriends. In fact, we can often recall those times when other details blur. For instance, you may not remember the classes you took in your senior year, but you probably still smile about the graduation party you and your girlfriends had or the friends who, with love and ice cream, healed a heart broken by someone whose name you can't recall. The scary days you spent by a sick parent's or child's bedside may have mercifully blurred, except for the loving faces of your girlfriends who brought comfort and great food (and made sure you ate something). Our lives would be a fuzzy dash from one obligation to another if we didn't pause momentarily and mark our accomplishments, explore our challenges, and share our day-to-day circumstances with our girlfriends.

In this book, we seek to honor the time we spend with our valuable friends. We don't mean to imply that there is a right or wrong way to have a "girlfriend get together," or that any gathering has to be a stressful production. We have found that most friends really don't care what they do together, so long as they have a chance to connect with one another. But we dare to "gild the lily"—offering in this book some suggestions that we hope will help you celebrate or honor some of the milestones—large and small, good and bad—in our lives.

Please consider all of these events as suggestions, which may trigger your own ideas. As a creative woman, you'll undoubtedly want to customize our ideas to fit your situation. So mix and match (or delete) recipes, pare down an event or make it more elaborate, create your own party favors and decorating ideas. The idea is to have fun.

Perhaps our most important suggestion is to do what you naturally do with your friends—relax! Most of us have had the experience of planning for a party—even a small one—only to be so exhausted by the preparation that we had no energy left to enjoy the actual event. We've included some "plan ahead" schedules for the more elaborate events to help you avoid that problem. And if something goes wrong, it is all fodder for your personal girlfriends legends, and, well let's face it, not one of your friends is really going to care! Creating an atmosphere of love and acceptance, not the perfect execution of every detail, is all you need for a successful gathering. Women are amazing creatures, and when you get us together in one room—expect the unexpected, the hilarious and outrageous, the meaningful and courageous. We hope *girlfriends get together* enriches these moments, and helps create more memories that you wouldn't give up for *anything*.

Chapters

Women in the Wild

Females of all ages love to run in packs in the outdoors, whether we're teenagers on a nocturnal trek to spy on some boy's house, young women stuffing eight of us into a tent made for four on a camping trip, or grown-ups invading an urban mall on the hunt for the perfect pumps. We are our best selves when we're *en masse*, tapping into ancient wild women energy that often lies dormant when we're on our own. An outdoor annual Women in the Wild get together is the perfect way to celebrate our kindred vibrancy at the end of a dusty trail, in the comfort of our backyards, or at the close of a tough week. So kick off your shoes, feel the grass beneath your feet, and gather the sisters around for some scrumptious treats.

Menu

GRILLED WILD AND DOMESTIC MUSHROOMS
WITH HERB BUTTER*

SPICED CORN-ON-THE-COB*

MARINATED AND GRILLED BUTTERFLIED
CORNISH GAME HENS*

ROASTED NEW POTATOES*

MARINATED AND GRILLED FLANK STEAK*

FRESH TOMATOES, GREEN BEANS

BREAD, BUTTER, ASSORTED CHEESES

FRESH FIGS, APRICOTS, AND MELON

PEACH-BLUEBERRY CRISP*

IMPORTED BEERS, WINE SPRITZERS, SPARKLING
WATER, AND SOFT DRINKS

GRILLED WILD AND DOMESTIC MUSHROOMS WITH HERB BUTTER

Makes 6 to 8 servings.

Herb Butter:

8 tablespoons unsalted butter
(4 ounces), softened

2½ tablespoons fresh Italian parsley, finely
chopped

2 tablespoons each finely chopped fresh basil
and chives

1½ teaspoons minced fresh thyme

Grilled Mushrooms:

2 very large portobella mushrooms
(about 1 pound), cleaned and quartered

1 pound domestic mushrooms, cleaned

1 pound shiitake mushrooms, cleaned
and stemmed

½ pound chanterelle or other wild mushrooms,
cleaned

Salt and pepper, to taste

Prepare the herb butter: In a small bowl combine the butter and herbs; mix well. May be kept in the refrigerator tightly covered for up to 3 days.

Prepare a charcoal grill. When the coals are medium hot (covered with a medium-thick layer of gray ash through which a red glow is visible), place the mushrooms on the grill and cook 15 to 20 minutes, rotating frequently to

Cooking Tip

* A wide assortment of wild mushrooms would be sensational for this dish, but if all you can find is domestic button and portobella mushrooms, don't worry! All mushrooms taste great when grilled over an open fire and brushed with herb butter. To remove the shiitake stem, use your thumb and forefinger to gently pull it from the cap; it will come out in one piece.

Remember that midnight picnic...

My friends love my back porch—it's where I can be found all summer! It is nestled in the midst of our one-acre wooded lot. One night my friend and I, and our daughters, were having a wonderful time chatting and laughing. All of a sudden, we felt starved! It was very late, so we had to find an all-night grocery store. We bought every kind of appetizer and snack imaginable! Then we rushed home. While the appetizers were baking, we turned on the miniature white lights on the porch and lit every candle we could find. We set up a huge smorgasbord with our treats. There we were at one o'clock in the morning with the dark forest all around us, surrounded by light and food and friendship. We still say, "Remember that midnight picnic on the back porch?"

Sue

GRILLED MUSHROOMS (CONTINUED)

cook evenly. Cooking time will differ among the mushroom varieties because they vary in size and moisture content. Remove mushrooms as they become soft and aromatic, transferring them to a large platter. Immediately brush with the butter and season with salt and pepper.

Food is an important part of a balanced diet.

Fran Lebowitz
Metropolitan Life (1978)

SPICED
CORN-ON-THE-COB

Feel free to slather butter all over your corn once it comes off the grill; however, the sweet-savory spice blend and vegetable oil produce a terrific flavor.

Makes 8 servings.

2 teaspoons ground coriander

1½ teaspoons chili powder

1 teaspoon each Kosher salt and sugar

¼ teaspoon mace

Juice from one lime

3 tablespoons corn or vegetable oil

8 large ears corn, cleaned

In a small bowl, combine the coriander, chili powder, salt, sugar, mace, lime juice, and oil; mix well. Place corn on individual pieces of aluminum foil large enough to wrap each ear in a double-thick layer of foil. Brush with the spice mixture and wrap tightly.

Prepare a charcoal grill. When the coals are hot (red glowing coals covered with a very thin layer of gray ash), place the corn on the edge of the grill and cook 30 to 35 minutes, rotating frequently to cook evenly. Check occasionally for doneness. Exact time will vary depending on intensity of fire and size of corn. Remove from grill when done and serve immediately.

Who knew?

Although many of us have struggled with the inconspicuous removal of impertinent kernels stuck in our teeth, we did not realize, until reading Amy Vanderbilt's *Everyday Etiquette* (the 1956 edition), that corn-on-the-cob presents considerable challenges to polite eating. Of the many rules included therein, we present some of the highlights here:

• You MAY break the cob in half.

• You MAY NOT butter and season the whole ear at once, but only a row or so a time.

•You MAY concoct a mixture of salt-and-pepper to season the corn, but only if it is piled unnoticeably on the edge of the plate.

• You MAY NOT roll the corn in the salt and pepper mixture but only apply it with a knife a little at a time.

• You MAY cut the kernels off the cob with a knife, but only if the cob is held on one end with the left hand and the kernels cut off a few rows at a time with the dinner knife.

Modern etiquette mavens tell us that it is okay to eat corn with our fingers, but buttering and salting should only be done a few rows at a time to keep the messiness to a minimum. Emily Post would clearly like to eliminate corn on the cob altogether, but reluctantly instructs: "[I]f you insist on eating [corn-on-the-cob] at home or in a restaurant, to attack it with as little ferocity as possible, is perhaps the only direction to be given, since at best it is an ungraceful performance and to eat it greedily a horrible sight!" Isn't it a relief to know that we do not need to be so formal with our girlfriends?

How do I know when it's done?

* **Green Beans** If you are merely steaming some green beans, you can check for doneness by color (it is a bright, clover green) and by flexibility— a well-cooked bean will bend slightly but break crisply before it can be bent in half.

* **Corn-on-the-Cob** Corn is done cooking when a bit of "corn juice" squirts out of a kernel when poked with a fork tine.

One cannot think well, love well, sleep well, if one has not dined well.

Virginia Woolf
A Room of One's Own (1929)

MARINATED AND GRILLED BUTTERFLIED CORNISH GAME HENS

Cornish game hens are usually sold alongside chicken in the poultry section of the grocery store. If you're unsure of how to butterfly the hen, ask your butcher to do it for you.
Makes 6 to 8 servings.

4 Cornish game hens (7 to 8 pounds total), butterflied

Marinade:

2 cups orange juice

⅓ cup vegetable oil

⅓ cup tomato sauce

¼ cup honey

2 teaspoons ground coriander

6 cloves garlic, minced

Place each butterflied Cornish game hen in a heavy, durable plastic bag. In a medium bowl, combine the marinade ingredients, stirring with a whisk to form a smooth emulsion. Pour the marinade over the hens, dividing it equally among the four bags. Seal bags tightly and place in a large, shallow container (in case the bags leak slightly) in the refrigerator overnight or for 24 hours.

To roast wonderful potatoes

* Ever wish you knew how restaurants achieve those creamy-on-the-inside, crunchy-on-the-outside roast potatoes? We recommend roasting potatoes the following way: Use Yukon Gold potatoes, which have thin skins and a creamy texture. After washing them and patting them dry, cut them into the size you like. We recommend a chunky size akin to lemon wedges—if you cut them too small, the roasting will create hard, tough little nuggets, and cutting them too big will make them difficult to cook through without drying out the exterior. Whether or not you leave the skins on the potatoes is a matter of taste; we prefer them.

* After cutting the potato pieces, put them in a bowl and coat them with some olive oil (about one or two tablespoons per pound of potatoes—it does not take much), salt and pepper them lightly, and put them in a 425-degree oven, on a baking sheet or in a pan that has been lightly oiled or greased. Cook for about half an hour, turning two or three times to keep them from sticking to the pan. Serve immediately.

Roughing It...

I have a friend, Betty, for whom good food is always a priority in our gatherings. Once when we were about eighteen years old, Betty and I and two other friends went camping. We had very little camping equipment, but thanks to Betty, we had New York steaks, superbly seasoned and cooked on the campfire grill with sautéed vegetables, baked potatoes, and garlic butter. Before the night was over, we made lots of friends from the neighboring campsites and traded food and beer for such "nonessentials" as flashlights, toothpaste, and cooking pots.

Sherry

CORNISH GAME HENS
(CONTINUED)

Prepare a charcoal grill. When the coals are medium hot (covered with a medium-thick layer of gray ash through which a red glow is visible), place the hens, skin-side down, on the grill and cook approximately 20 minutes, rotating frequently for even cooking until juices run clear when meat is pierced next to the bone. Exact cooking time will vary depending on intensity of fire and size of hens. Do not overcook. Remove from grill and let stand 10 minutes before serving.

Somehow everything always tastes better when eaten outdoors on a warm evening, accompanied by great wine and great company!

Wynn McClenahan Burkett
Author

MARINATED AND GRILLED FLANK STEAK

The combination of salty, tangy, and sweet flavors in this marinade add an enticing flavor to grilled meat.

Makes about 8 servings.

2 pounds flank steak, trimmed of excess fat

Marinade:

3 tablespoons teriyaki sauce

3 tablespoons vegetable or light olive oil

2 tablespoons prepared mustard

2 tablespoons maple syrup

3 cloves garlic, minced

2 teaspoons each paprika and crushed sage leaves

1 teaspoon ground thyme

Salt and pepper, to taste

Place the steak in a large, shallow container (glass, stainless steel, or ceramic) large enough to accommodate it in one layer. In a small bowl, combine the remaining ingredients; mix well. Spread marinade over both sides of the steak. Cover tightly and refrigerate for 24 hours.

Prepare a charcoal grill. When the coals are hot (red glowing coals covered with a very thin layer of gray ash), place steak on grill and cook 10 to 12 minutes for medium doneness, rotating frequently to cook evenly. Season with salt and pepper. Remove steak from grill and let stand for 10 minutes before slicing.

Cooking Tip

* To keep the edges of steak from curling during grilling, use kitchen shears (or a very sharp knife) to make ½-inch-deep cuts every 2 inches around the edge of the meat.

Wild Woman Decorations

Women in groups often become a little bolder, a little less conservative than when they are alone. If you and your friends are feeling like "letting your hair down" in the outdoors, try some of the following:

* string some beads for anklets

* pin flowers in your hair

* apply temporary body tattoos with stamps and washable ink

Remember when applying temporary tattoos, the focus is on *washable* ink! Last summer some of our friends ended up wearing long-sleeved shirts and dark stockings to their very conservative offices after returning from a day at the beach (and stamping *permanent* ink on their bodies)!

Planning your outdoors event

The whole point of entertaining is for everyone to enjoy themselves. When hosting a party for your friends, the procrastinators among us can get a bit behind in the plans, and end up doing everything at the last minute! Anyone who has been in this situation knows the difficulty of enjoying an evening when you have had to cram in all the preparations that day. When throwing a party for your girlfriends, you can always ask them to help (likely they will insist on it). But when you want to put on a special outdoors event at home, for your friends and without their assistance, we suggest the following party countdown schedule. It will reduce stress and allow you to be relaxed and spend quality time with your valued guests.

- PARTY MINUS SEVEN TO TEN DAYS Telephone your friends with an invitation.
- PARTY MINUS THREE DAYS Buy all the ingredients for the recipes except for the tomatoes and bread.
- PARTY MINUS TWO DAYS Make sure you have all the serving dishes, napkins, plates, glasses, and cutlery you will need. Do you need any citronella candles to keep the mosquitoes away?
- PARTY MINUS ONE DAY Marinate the Cornish game hens and flank steak and refrigerate. Prepare the spice blend for the corn-on-the-cob (don't put it on the corn yet) and refrigerate. Make the peach-blueberry crisp and refrigerate.
- PARTY DAY Earlier in the day, buy ripe tomatoes and fresh, crusty bread, and prepare the remaining food as much as possible before your guests arrive. Assemble all the eating utensils and serving pieces in one place in preparation for taking outside. Put any white wine or other drinks that should be chilled in the refrigerator, and if you are preparing any special mixed drinks, prepare enough to have a pitcherful ready about half an hour before your guests arrive. Later, as you prepare your grill, remember that the mushrooms and Cornish game hens should be cooked first over a medium-hot grill, then the flank steak and the corn-on-the-cob, which should be cooked over a hot grill. Turn your oven down to 300 degrees F after taking out the potatoes and warm the peach-blueberry crisp during dinner. While you are grilling, let your guests help you bring the remaining food outside. Enjoy!

PEACH-BLUEBERRY CRISP

Makes 8 to 10 servings.

8 large peaches, pitted and cut into 1½-inch pieces

1 pint blueberries, stemmed if necessary

½ cup sugar

¼ cup fresh lemon juice

⅓ cup cornstarch (use ¼ cup if you like the fruit portion a little runnier)

1½ cups all-purpose flour

1½ cups old-fashioned oats

1¼ cups light brown sugar

1½ tablespoons cinnamon

16 tablespoons (8 ounces) chilled, unsalted butter, cut into ½-inch chunks

Cooking Tip

★ The key to making the dessert topping crisp and crumbly is to use a light touch when mixing the butter into the dry ingredients, and by sprinkling it on the fruit just before baking.

Generously grease a 13 x 9 x 2-inch (3-quart) baking pan. In a large bowl, combine the peaches, blueberries, sugar, and lemon juice; mix well. Let stand at room temperature for 1 hour, stirring occasionally.

Preheat oven to 350 degrees F. Sprinkle the cornstarch over the fruit mixture and mix well, taking care to dissolve any small lumps. Transfer to a prepared baking dish. In a medium bowl, combine the flour, oats, light brown sugar, and cinnamon; mix thoroughly. Add the butter in chunks. Using your fingers or two knives, cut the butter into the dry ingredients until the mixture resembles coarse bread crumbs (some pea-size bits of butter should remain visible). Do not overmix or the topping will be stiff and dry. Using your fingers, loosely sprinkle the topping evenly over fruit. Do not press it onto the fruit.

PEACH-BLUEBERRY CRISP
(CONTINUED)

Place on lower shelf of preheated oven and bake 35 minutes. Move to upper shelf and bake 10 to 15 more minutes, or until topping is dark golden brown and fruit is bubbly. Remove from oven and let cool to room temperature before cutting into serving pieces.

Outdoor Memories

Include here pictures or stories of your favorite time with your girlfriends in the outdoors—remember that the outdoors includes your backyard and the terrace of your favorite restaurant!

Friday Night Film Fest

Let your hair down—the workweek is over and an entire weekend is just beginning. Who better to gripe about your job, gossip about your romances, and compare weekend plans with than your girlfriends? After you slough off the week's troubles and dive into some tasty finger food, get ready to slouch on the couch and watch some favorite films. Thank goodness it's Friday!

Menu

CHIPOTLE JUMBO PRAWNS*

SHAVED JICAMA WITH FRESH LIME*

HOT SHOTS (CHEESE-STUFFED JALAPENO CHILI PEPPERS)*

NACHOS WITH BLACK BEANS*

TORTILLA CHIPS WITH SALSA VERDE*
AND ANCHO CHILI–TOMATO SALSA*

BITTERSWEET CHOCOLATE–ALMOND TORTE*

STIRRED MARGARITAS, PINEAPPLE-MANGO DAIQUIRIS, AND ASSORTED
MEXICAN BEERS AND SOFT DRINKS

CHIPOTLE JUMBO PRAWNS

Chipotle chilies are dried and smoked fresh jalapeno peppers. They have a unique and wonderful flavor and pack a tremendous jolt of fire. They are sold packed in sauce in small cans, or in dry form in bulk. If you find them sold in plastic bags in dry form, simply soak in cold water until soft and pliable. Remove stems and seeds, then mince with a sharp knife or cut into tiny pieces using kitchen shears.

To avoid skin contact with these hot chilies, instead use canned chipotle chili peppers in adobe sauce, found in all Latin American food stores and in most Mexican food sections of your grocery store.

Makes about 6 servings.

2 pounds jumbo prawns, shelled and tails removed

1½ to 2 tablespoons minced chipotle chili pepper

1 teaspoon each ground coriander and cayenne pepper

½ teaspoon ground cumin

2 cloves garlic, minced

Cooking Tip

* Some raw chilies may irritate your skin when handling them. Make sure you wash your hands with hot water and soap after handling. And do not rub your eyes!

A tip about party plans
Suit Yourself!

Modify any party plans to suit your own needs. The best hosts know when to limit what they do and realize that simplicity allows them to retain their sanity while truly enjoying their guests. So cut the number of recipes, replace them if you want, do whatever will suit your time limits and budget. Do the things you choose to do well, and no one will know what you chose not to do. If you are working and single, you can take heart in this passage directed to "career girls" from *You, Too, Can Be The Perfect Hostess*, written in 1950: "We're not concerned with the

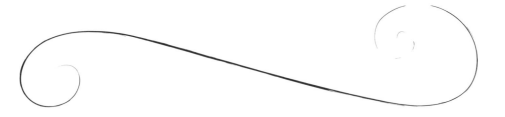

size of your apartment or the size of your income. Actually, neither matters very much when it comes to entertaining attractively. The career girl has a distinct advantage over her married sisters, because she can get by with all sorts of entertaining shortcuts (people don't expect elaborate preparations from a gal who throws a party at the end of a busy business day). And because you, the working girl, can get by with extremely simple, casual forms of entertaining at home, your parties should be that much more relaxed, informal and fun." Of course, there is no neat delineation between "career girls" and their "married sisters" these days (everyone has such busy lives!), but her point is well taken: Make sure you are having fun too—you will be the better host for it!

CHIPOTLE JUMBO PRAWNS (CONTINUED)

Place prawns and remaining ingredients in a medium bowl, mix well. Cover tightly and refrigerate for at least 6 hours, or up to 24.

Preheat the broiler portion of the oven. Use 6 or 8 stainless steel skewers each 12 inches long. Thread the prawns onto the skewers end-to-end so they lay flat. When the broiler is hot (about 15 minutes), place the prawns under the broiler and cook 2 to 3 minutes on the first side. Flip over and cook the second side about 2 minutes, or until prawns are just cooked throughout. Do not overcook. Remove from broiler and serve immediately.

I just hate health food.

Julia Child

SALSA VERDE

This recipe is very easy to make and far better than the store-bought version. If you have leftover salsa, use it as a sauce for grilled or roasted chicken and fish.

Makes about 4 cups.

1 pound tomatillas, husks removed

4 large jalapeno chili peppers, stemmed, halved and seeded

1 cup loosely packed cilantro leaves

6 scallions, trimmed and coarsely chopped

Salt and pepper, to taste

In a large pot, bring 4 quarts of water to boil over high heat. Add the tomatillas and jalapenos. Return to a boil and cook 3 to 4 minutes, or until the tomatillas are just tender. Drain well and refresh with cold running water.

Using a blender, puree in batches the tomatillas and chilies, and a little of the cooking liquid, plus the cilantro and scallions until ground. Remove from blender and transfer to a serving dish. Season with salt and pepper; mix well and serve immediately. Will keep for up to 4 days stored in a tightly sealed plastic, glass, stainless steel, or ceramic container in the refrigerator.

The origin of Nachos

Apparently there is some controversy over whether nachos were created in America or Mexico. According to Cheryl Alters Jamison and Bill Jamison in *The Border Cookbook: Authentic Home Cooking of the American Southwest and Northern Mexico*, the specific origin is not known: "All that's certain is a Rio Grande origin about fifty years ago—and an inventor blessed with insight into the elemental." However, according to Adriana P. Orr, a twenty-five-year researcher for the *Oxford English Dictionary*, who spent a considerable amount of time researching the etymology of the word *nacho*, this delectable dish was created by Ignacio Anaya, a chef at the Victory Club in Piedras Negras (a Mexican town just across the border from Eagle Pass, Texas), and first served by him in 1943 to some Eagle Pass ladies who were in town for a shopping trip. (Ms. Orr also found that, in Mexico, *nacho* is a diminutive for a little boy who had been baptized Ignacio.) Whatever the source, nachos are a wonderful "food canvas"—you can put anything on them and they will taste great! When we first saw nachos as a dish, they consisted of melting Monterey Jack cheese over some tortilla pieces and sprinkling the mix with some sliced jalapenos. As nachos evolved (or some may say devolved), we see them piled with refried beans, jack cheese, salsa, guacamole, jalapenos, and sour cream—a delightfully goopy and caloric mix. For something a bit lighter, you may wish to substitute black beans (you can buy them canned) for the refried beans, add some shredded chicken, feta cheese, and chopped mangoes and drizzle with salsa verde.

Did you know...

* October 21 is the International Day of the Nacho.

HOT SHOTS

Fresh chili peppers vary in heat, so it's hard to know how incendiary your Hot Shots will be until you take your first bite. Not to worry, though—if they turn out to be a little too hot for some, there's always relief in the form of a couple spoonfuls of yogurt, or a bit or two of plain rice or bread.

Makes about 4 to 6 servings.

16 very large medium–dark green jalapeno chili peppers (3½ to 4 inches long and about 1 inche around)

4 to 6 ounces smoked Monterey Jack cheese, cut into ⅛-by-3½-inch-long strips

4 to 6 ounces medium Cheddar cheese, cut into ⅛-by-3½-inch-long strips

In a large saucepan, bring 1 quart of water to boil over high heat. Add chili peppers and cook 2 minutes. Drain in colander and refresh with cold water. Transfer to a bowl filled with ice water and let stand until thoroughly chilled.

Preheat oven to 350 degrees F. Using a paring knife, on each chili pepper make a ½-inch-long incision across the pepper just under the stem. Starting at the right side of the incision, cut lengthwise down the pepper making one side of a V-shaped cut approximately 1 inch long. Return to the left side of the cross-wise incision and make a second V-shaped cut to form a triangle. Gently remove the triangle section of chili and the seeds and discard both. Take care not to tear the chili pepper. Pat the inside with paper towels to remove any remaining seeds and excess moisture. Stuff each chili pepper with strips of both kinds of cheese. Place on lightly greased cookie sheet or pie tins and bake 12 to 15 minutes, or until cheese is just melted. Remove from oven and serve immediately.

ANCHO CHILI— TOMATO SALSA

All Latin American food markets and most large grocery stores carry a wide variety of dried chili peppers, sold in bulk or packaged in small plastic bags.

Makes about 3½ cups.

3 dried ancho chili peppers

3 New Mexico dried chili peppers

½ onion, thinly sliced

2 cloves garlic, thinly sliced

7 roma tomatoes, thinly sliced lengthwise

1 cup cold water

½ bunch cilantro, stemmed and coarsely chopped

Salt and pepper, to taste

Soak the dried chilies in cold water to cover until soft. Remove stems and seeds and place in blender. Set aside until needed.

In a large, heavy-bottomed, nonstick sauté pan, cook the onion, garlic, and tomatoes over high heat 8 to 10 minutes, stirring frequently, until the onions are charred and the tomatoes are blackened on all sides. Add the water and mix well. Add the mixture (including the water) to the blender, along with the cilantro. Puree until smooth. Season with salt and pepper and serve. Will keep for up to 5 days in a tightly sealed plastic, glass, ceramic, or stainless steel container stored in the refrigerator.

About Jicama

* According to *Webster's*, jicama is "an edible, starchy tuberous root of a leguminous tropical American vine." That description may not sound so appetizing, but jicama is actually a very tasty legume, with high water content and a lovely crunchy texture. It serves as a perfect complement to spicy and peppery dishes. To prepare it, peel the jicama with a sharp paring knife and then shred with a grater or slice into very thin pieces with a chef's knife. Drizzle lime juice over it and before you know it, you will have an easy, juicy side dish for your Mexican meal.

Creating your Filmfest

You can pick a theme for your Friday Night Film Fest, such as:

- ## BABE-O-RAMA NIGHT

  Includes any movie starring Cary Grant, Mel Gibson, Denzel Washington, George Clooney, Tyrone Power, Will Smith, Ben Affleck, Matt Damon, Leonardo DiCaprio, or the babe of your choice (and any combination of the above).

- ## WOMEN SOLIDARITY NIGHT

  Includes *Fried Green Tomatoes, Thelma and Louise, Pride and Prejudice, Beaches, The Joy Luck Club, Antonia and Jane, Romy and Michelle's High School Reunion, First Wives Club, Enchanted April, Boys on the Side, Waiting to Exhale, Charlie's Angels, Miss Congeniality* (and don't forget re-runs of *Xena: Warrior Princess*).

- ## TRUE LOVE STILL EXISTS

  Includes *An Affair to Remember, Sleepless in Seattle, Roxanne, The Goodbye Girl, Titanic, Romeo and Juliet,* and *The Philadelphia Story* (there are many to choose from in this category).

- ## I HATE MY JOB

  Includes *9 to 5* and *Working Girl*.

You get the idea!

BITTERSWEET CHOCOLATE–ALMOND TORTE

This luscious, rich torte is divine served alone, but if you want to really "gild the lily," serve with a dollop of slightly sweetened whipped cream or high-quality vanilla ice cream. Makes 6 to 8 servings.

1 cup whole almonds

¾ cup sugar

8 ounces bittersweet chocolate, broken into small pieces

8 tablespoons unsalted butter

5 eggs, separated

2 teaspoons vanilla extract

3 tablespoons all-purpose flour

Generously grease an 8½-inch springform pan. Preheat oven to 350 degrees F. Using a food processor, process the almonds and sugar until finely ground. Set aside until needed.

In the top of a double boiler, melt the chocolate and butter over moderately low heat, stirring occasionally. Remove from heat and cool to room temperature. In a large bowl, whisk together the egg yolks, vanilla extract, and flour to form a smooth mixture. Add the melted butter-chocolate mixture and mix well. Stir in almond-sugar mixture and mix well.

A Perfect Party Favor

In the "busyness" of our lives, we have given up on creating party favors for our guests, except for the most special occasions. But we have some easy suggestions for party favors that can add a little fun to even a casual Friday night gathering. To help your guests get settled in to watch a great movie:

* Hand out slipper sox to each guest to keep toes warm during the show.
* Give each girlfriend a name tag so she can write the name of a movie star she would most like to be.
* Serve your tortilla chips or nachos in individual boxes or buckets, just like popcorn is served at the movies.

All Aboard

Thirty years ago, as single starving artists in New York City, my friends and I were forever inventing ways to celebrate the end of the workweek without blowing our meager budgets. After exhausting our lists of free, all-you-can-eat buffets offered at upscale bars' happy hours, we stumbled upon the ultimate "Jack Benny Night on the Town." We learned that cruise ships charged only fifty cents to board during the predeparture period. Our favorite Friday night ritual became the free bon voyage parties, especially those aboard the *Queen Elizabeth II*. We mingled with affluent passengers while sipping champagne and nibbling on fancy finger food. It was the survival of the fittest!

Ellen

BITTERSWEET CHOCOLATE— ALMOND TORTE (CONTINUED)

In a small, deep bowl, using an electric mixer, whip the egg whites until stiff peaks form. Fold one-third of the egg whites into the batter and mix gently. Add remaining whites and gently stir until almost blended. A few streaks of egg whites ought to remain. Pour batter into prepared pan and bake on the bottom shelf of the oven 30 to 35 minutes. The center will still be soft. Check for doneness by inserting a toothpick into the torte about 1 inch from the outside. Remove from oven and let stand at room temperature until cool. Slice into serving pieces and garnish with whipped cream. Store at room temperature, covered with plastic wrap, for up to 3 days.

Artur has his piano. I play my sonatas on the stove.

Nella Rubinstein

Just Talk

We don't have to be on our best behavior, or in the best mood, to hang out with our girlfriends. On the contrary—when disappointment, confusion, or sheer loneliness interrupts our happiness, we turn to our friends for encouragement, wise advice, and simple companionship. If you're feeling like you need to talk, or would prefer to say nothing and just soak up the comforting presence of women who love and understand you, invite a girlfriend or two over and serve up this easy menu. Or prepare this meal for a friend who could use an attentive ear. You'll all feel better very soon.

Menu

OPEN-FACED ITALIAN MELT ON SOURDOUGH*

ZUCCHINI–BELL PEPPER SLAW*

ASSORTED OLIVES

ICE CREAM WITH CARAMEL AND CHOCOLATE SAUCES

WINE AND SPARKLING WATER

OPEN-FACED ITALIAN MELT ON SOURDOUGH

The intoxicating aroma of sweet, caramelized onions is inviting, and the flavor—irresistible. You may want to make a batch to keep on hand for adding to pasta, rice, vegetable dishes, or as an accompaniment to meat or poultry. If you can't find Walla Walla or other sweet onions, use 8 or 9 yellow or white onions instead. Makes 4 sandwiches.

6 large Walla Walla or other sweet onions, halved and thinly sliced

4 large tomatoes, thinly sliced

1 pound Havarti, Fontina, or Gouda cheese (or other mild melting cheese), thinly sliced

4 large sourdough rolls or 1-pound sourdough loaf

In a very large, nonstick sauté pan, cook half of the onions over high heat 7 or 8 minutes, stirring frequently until wilted and golden brown. Transfer to bowl and set aside. Cook remaining onions in same fashion until wilted and golden brown. Add the first batch of onions to those in the sauté pan and cook over moderate heat 25 to 30 minutes, stirring occasionally, until very soft, deep brown, and aromatic. Remove from heat and cool to room temperature.

Preheat oven to 400 degrees F. To make one sandwich, slice roll in half or slice bread into 8 2½-by-3½-inch pieces. Use about ⅔ cup of onions per sandwich; spread evenly on cut side of bread. Cover onions with tomato slices and

Menopause and Memory Loss

For several years now, eight of us have been getting together monthly. We call ourselves the Menopause and Memory Loss Support Group (and Dinner Society). We initially gathered at a restaurant, but now at each other's houses for a potluck brunch or dinner. We all know each other from many years back and some of us see each other regularly, some only intermittently, and some don't get together outside of the M&M gatherings. Some of us are lesbian and some are straight, some have children and some don't, most are working but one has just retired, some are single and some are in relationships. Several have recently split up with long-term partners and are "playing the field" (with some success—who says women over the age of forty, or in this case, fifty, can't find partners?). We talk, laugh, compare notes about the menopausal experiences we are having (once we compared medications), pick on anyone who forgets anything, and jump on anyone who says "What?" (hearing loss!)—all in fun. We celebrate birthdays with lots of silly greeting cards about the foibles of the elderly, share vacation photos, talk some politics. But the serious side is that we listen to each other and support each other through crises like aging and sick parents, difficult children, brushes with cancer, career choices, partners, and even one case of a lodger-from-hell.

Laura

OPEN-FACED ITALIAN
MELT ON SOURDOUGH
(CONTINUED)

top tomatoes with cheese. Place open-faced sandwiches on cookie sheet or pie tins and bake in oven 5 to 7 minutes, or until the cheese is just melted. Serve immediately.

*Each person's life is lived
as a series of conversations.*

Deborah Tannen
You Just Don't Understand (1990)

ZUCCHINI–BELL PEPPER SLAW

Raw summer squash and bell peppers lend a fresh, healthful flavor to this colorful salad. This dish takes less than 15 minutes to prepare, so you can make it at the last minute without stressing. Because the zucchini tends to wilt with time, it's actually best served the same day. Makes 4 servings.

2 medium-sized green zucchini, cut on the diagonal into 1½-inch-long skinny strips

2 yellow zucchini, cut on the diagonal into 1½-inch-long skinny strips

1 large red bell pepper, sliced into 1½-inch-long skinny strips

2 cloves garlic, minced

½ teaspoon each ground fennel seed and oregano

2 tablespoons olive oil

1 tablespoon white wine vinegar

Salt and pepper, to taste

Finely chopped parsley, for garnish

In a large bowl, combine the green and yellow zucchini, bell pepper, garlic, fennel seed, oregano, olive oil, and vinegar. Season with salt and pepper and mix well. Serve immediately, garnished with parsley.

Girls' Night Out...

As a newcomer to the neighborhood, I was invited to join a "Girls' Night Out" group. We met at a different home monthly for refreshments, camaraderie, and a chance to work on needlepoint projects. Best of all, we laughed and let off a lot of steam. Some likened it to a "stitch and bitch" club, but it was actually great suburban therapy.

Ellen

A smiling face is half the meal.

Latvian proverb

Speaking into the perforations of a telephone receiver as if through the screen of a confessional, we do sometimes share our emotions with a friend, but usually this is too disembodied, too much like yelling into the wind. We prefer to talk in person, as if we could temporarily slide into their feelings. Our friend first offers food, drink. It is a symbolic act, a gesture that says: This food will nourish your body as I will nourish your soul.

Diane Ackerman
A Natural History of the Senses (1990)

My Good Friends

Can you remember a time when a friend has lent you her ear?

Memories and Notes

Photos

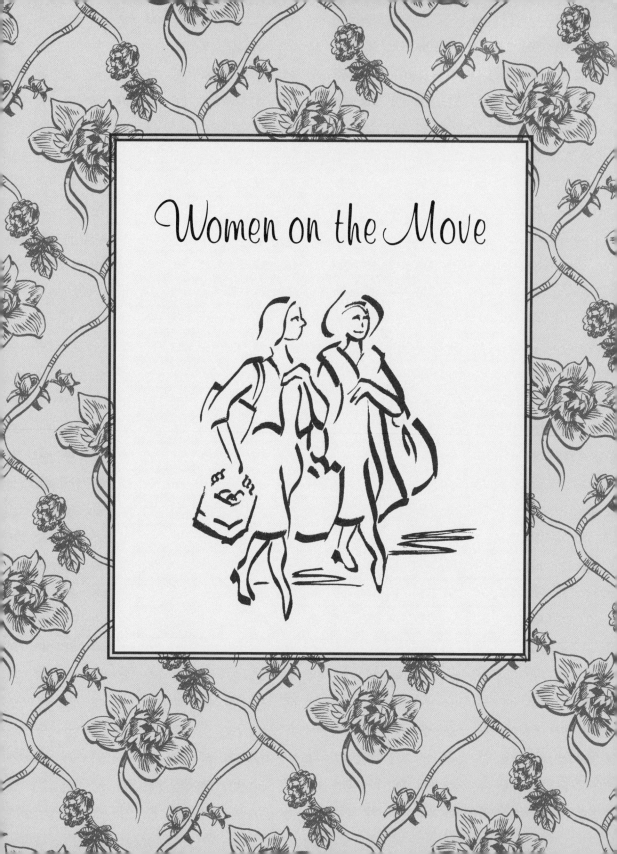

Women on the Move

Chapters

Moving Day Picnic

Boxes as far as the eye can see, and after an hour of searching, you still cannot find the one with your underwear. Thank goodness for your trusted girlfriends, because who else would you want going through your private belongings? When we're in transition from one home to another, we can count on our friends to put new shelving paper in the kitchen, unpack our sweaters and sort them by season and color, and give an opinion as to where to hang our pictures. Reward their hard work with a hearty meal, easy to make but worthy of girlfriends' loyalty. If your friend is the one moving, this is a terrific carry-in lunch to eat on top of the boxes or on the front stoop.

Menu

TURKEY ROLLS WITH BELL PEPPERS*

HUMMUS PITA POCKETS WITH CUCUMBERS AND TOMATOES*

HERB-GARLIC–STUFFED MUSHROOMS*

BREAD STICKS AND/OR BAGEL CHIPS

LEMON BARS*

TURKEY ROLLS WITH BELL PEPPERS

To add a fourth color to these edible mosaics, cut carrots into the same size as the bell peppers and cook in boiling water 1 minute or until crisp-tender. Drain well and dry on towels before using in the rolls.

Makes 14 to 16 rolls, about 8 servings.

¾ pound cream cheese, softened

¼ cup minced chives

1 clove garlic, minced

1 pound thinly sliced turkey, 14 to 16 slices

1 large red bell pepper, cut into strips approximately ⅛ inch by 3 inches

1 large yellow bell pepper, cut into strips approximately ⅛ inch by 3 inches

1 large green bell pepper, cut into strips approximately ⅛ inch by 3 inches

In a medium bowl, combine the cream cheese, chives, and garlic; mix well. To make one roll, lay a slice of the turkey on a flat surface. Spread with a thin layer of the cream cheese mixture. Place 1 or 2 strips (depending on the total number of strips) of each color bell pepper at one end of turkey. Begin rolling, taking care to make a tight, neat package. Make the remaining rolls in the same fashion. Slice the rolls in half and serve on a platter, cut-side up.

One Woman's Junk...

Moving and relocating, under any circumstances, can be a nightmare, especially if you have lived in the same home for thirty-four years. My family and I decided that every item in the house was to be categorized either yes or no, pack or trash. My two friends Lois and Mary decided that they were both going to help. Each took a large black trash bag, and whenever I threw something into the so-called "trash pile," it almost automatically became a treasure for one of my helpers. After several hours, I called it a day. Imagine Lois's surprise when she got home and discovered that in her zeal, she also managed to take home a "real" bag of trash!

Gloria

HUMMUS PITA POCKETS WITH CUCUMBERS AND TOMATOES

Makes 6 pita pockets.

Hummus:

3 cups cooked garbanzo beans

½ cup tahini

¼ cup olive oil

¼ to ⅓ cup fresh lemon juice

3 cloves garlic, finely chopped

¼ to ⅓ cup cold water

Dash cayenne pepper

Salt and pepper, to taste

6 whole wheat pita bread rounds

1 large English cucumber, peeled and
   thinly sliced

3 large tomatoes, thinly sliced

Cooking Tip

* It's always nice to make things from scratch when cooking, but in this hummus dish canned garbanzo beans work just as well as freshly cooked. Hummus can be made and used in the sandwiches right away, but the flavor becomes a little richer by the second and third day.

Using a food processor, place in the work bowl the garbanzo beans, tahini, olive oil, lemon juice, garlic, and water. Process until smooth and thoroughly mixed. Mixture should be the consistency of smooth peanut butter. If necessary, add a little more water or lemon juice to thin the hummus. Add the cayenne, salt, and pepper and process once again to combine.

Cut each pita round in half and open gently to form a pocket. Using about 5 tablespoons of hummus per half-pita, spread the inside of the bread with the hummus, taking care not to tear the bread. Place 5 or 6 cucumber slices inside, along with 2 or 3 tomato slices. Press gently to seal. Serve at room temperature.

HERB-GARLIC—
STUFFED MUSHROOMS

Stuffed mushrooms are traditionally served hot, but these are equally delicious served at room temperature. Look for jumbo-size mushrooms to stuff, and large mushrooms for chopping and using in the filling.
Makes 8 stuffed mushrooms.

8 jumbo mushrooms, cleaned with a kitchen towel

1¼ pounds button mushrooms, cleaned with a kitchen towel or washed and thoroughly dried

3 cloves garlic, minced

3 tablespoons unsalted butter

2 tablespoons olive oil

¼ cup finely chopped fresh parsley

¼ cup finely chopped fresh chives

1½ tablespoons minced fresh thyme

¾ cup finely ground plain bread crumbs

Salt and pepper, to taste

Prepare the mushrooms to be stuffed: Using a small spoon, gently remove (and reserve) the stem and scrape the brown portion from around the inside edge of the mushroom cap, taking care not to break the cap. Set mushroom caps aside until needed. Place the stems and scrapings on a cutting board, along with the button mushrooms, and finely chop.

Heaven Sent

When my mother died, I went back to the Midwest to sell the house and dispose of its contents. Being an only child whose father had died two years earlier meant all of the moving, selling, etc., was left up to me. I found myself feeling isolated and became reclusive and morose. One of my very best friends, Lisa, flew a thousand miles and stayed with me for an entire week in my parents' home. Lisa is very organized. She not only helped me decide what items I wanted to keep, but also arranged for movers and shipping, and organized the items to be donated, sold, or given to distant family members. Lisa kept me emotionally intact. She would hug me when I found something particularly poignant and laugh and, thankfully, force me to throw away truly hideous things that I then thought that I wanted. I otherwise would have paid large sums of money to move truly hideous objects across country (we're talking plastic flowers and clowns painted on velvet!). We got that entire house packed up and settled within one week. The items that I brought back are now incorporated into my own home. I am happy with the items that Lisa helped me choose to keep. In my mind, I often thank Lisa for being there and keeping me sane.

Patricia

A Perfect "Thank You!"

If you are the one who is being helped by your friends, here are some suggestions for an end-of-the-day "thank you" on moving day:

* Hire a massage therapist to come in at the end of the day for an hour or two and give everyone 15-minute back rubs.

* Give everyone soothing bath salts to soak in after the move.

* Write out or, using a desktop publishing program, create and print a variety of coupons that are redeemable for favors such as:

  A home-cooked meal

  One night baby-sitting

  One dusting and vacuuming session

Put the coupons in a basket and allow each girlfriend to select one as a thank-you for her help.

The Stinking Rose

* Nothing makes a house more welcoming than the smell of garlic cooking. If you are bringing the herb-garlic–stuffed mushrooms, prepare them at home up to the stage where they are ready for the oven. Then bake them in your friend's new home, filling her home with that delicious aroma.

STUFFED MUSHROOMS (CONTINUED)

In a large, nonstick sauté pan, cook the finely chopped mushrooms and garlic in the butter and olive oil over moderate heat 12 to 15 minutes, stirring occasionally, until most of the liquid has evaporated. Add the herbs and cook 2 minutes, stirring constantly. Remove from heat and transfer to a medium bowl. Cool slightly. Add bread crumbs, salt, and pepper and stir gently with a fork to combine.

Preheat oven to 400 degrees F. Using a small spoon, stuff each mushroom cap with the filling, making a rounded dome shape on each one. Place stuffed mushrooms on a cookie sheet or baking pan (with sides under ½-inch high). Bake 15 to 20 minutes, or until the mushrooms are tender and the filling is hot. Remove from oven and serve immediately or cool to room temperature.

LEMON BARS

After much experimenting, we've decided this recipe makes lemon bars with the most balanced flavor, luscious texture, and buttery bottom layer. The key to making a tender, delicate crust is to combine the ingredients with a light touch and gently pat the mixture into the baking pan.
Makes about 24 squares.

2 cups all-purpose flour

½ cup confectioners' sugar

¼ cup cornstarch

11 tablespoons unsalted butter,
   cut into pea-size chunks

2 tablespoons margarine, cut into small pieces

6 eggs

2¼ cups sugar

6 tablespoons all-purpose flour

1 cup fresh lemon juice

½ cup milk

Generously grease a 9-by-13-inch baking pan. In a medium bowl, thoroughly mix together the flour, confectioners' sugar, and cornstarch until no lumps remain. Add the butter and margarine and, using your fingertips, combine the fat with the dry ingredients until the mixture resembles coarsely ground bread crumbs. There should be tiny bits of butter still visible. Transfer to the prepared baking pan and very gently pat the mixture into the pan, making

Moving Night

I would never have been able to move out of my home of ten years to my new house if it weren't for my friend Tammy. She was raised by a family that moved a lot, whereas I am a nester and pack rat, and as moving day loomed it looked like I wouldn't make it. Tammy called and scheduled a number of Moving Nights, when she brought over food and wine and helped me do the hardest thing of all for me: throwing out all the junk I had accumulated over the years but didn't want to take along. One particularly fun Moving Night involved Tammy sorting through my treasure trove of paper shopping bags with handles and my drawers full of plastic margarine and other containers. During spirited negotiations reminiscent of the Middle East peace process, I made my heartfelt arguments to Tammy as to why I just had to keep that paper shopping bag from the Museum of Modern Art exhibition in 1976, and why my favorite plastic plates from frozen dinners I'd eaten in the eighties were perfect for microwaving food today. At one point, she turned to me and said: "OK, I'll let you keep that triangular Tupperware® container if we can find the lid, and because you've been so good, I'll throw in this extra large margarine container as well." She was a ruthless sorter and tosser, completely bossy and inflexible about what I could take with me, and we just laughed through the entire evening.

Cassandra

LEMON BARS
(CONTINUED)

one even layer. Refrigerate 45 minutes to 1 hour before baking.

Meanwhile, in a large bowl, whisk together the eggs and sugar until thoroughly combined. Sprinkle the flour over the surface and quickly whisk it into the mixture, taking care to make a smooth emulsion free of lumps. Add the lemon juice and milk and mix well. Set aside until needed.

Preheat oven to 350 degrees F. Bake crust on upper shelf approximately 30 minutes, or until golden brown. Remove from oven and reduce heat to 325 degrees F. Pour lemon mixture over hot crust. Return to oven and bake on upper shelf 20 to 25 minutes, or until the filling just barely shakes when jiggled. Remove from oven and cool on baking rack to room temperature. When cool, cut into serving squares and serve immediately. Will keep tightly covered with plastic wrap at room temperature for up to 2 days.

A Housewarming Dinner

A house is just a structure until love turns it into a home. Begin this new phase of your life by inviting special girlfriends to help initiate your new home with warmth, joy, and blessing. Allow their love to permeate each room so that this strange location can be transformed into home, sweet home.

Menu

POTATO-ONION BREAD*

MIXED GREENS WITH APPLES AND BLUE CHEESE*

HEARTY SMOKED HAM SOUP WITH LIMA BEANS*

CARROT CAKE WITH CREAM CHEESE FROSTING*

POTATO-ONION BREAD

Be sure to bring all ingredients to room temperature before making the bread. A double rising as this recipe describes is preferable, but if you're pressed for time, skip the second rising and proceed with the directions for shaping and baking after the first rising. This savory bread is delicious plain, but we think it's even better cut into thick slices, warmed in the oven, and slathered with lots of sweet butter.
Makes 1 large loaf, about 8 servings.

2 packages (¼-ounce) dry yeast

⅓ cup water, 110 to 115 degrees F

5-plus cups bread flour

1 cup dried potato flakes

1 bunch scallions, green portion only, finely chopped

2 tablespoons dried onions

2 tablespoons sugar

2 tablespoons kosher salt

2 cups cottage cheese, room temperature

4 tablespoons unsalted butter, melted (and still warm)

1 egg, lightly beaten

Alone…and so am I, if a choice must be made between most people I know and myself. This misanthropic attitude is one I am not proud of, but it is firmly there, based on my increasing conviction that sharing food with another human being is an intimate act that should not be indulged in lightly.

M.F.K. Fisher
An Alphabet for Gourmets (1949)

Combine the yeast and water in a small bowl and let stand until the yeast is dissolved. Meanwhile, combine in a large bowl the bread flour, potato flakes, scallions, dried onions, sugar, and salt; mix well. Make a well in the center of the dry ingredients. Add the yeast mixture, along with the cottage cheese, butter, and egg. Using your index and middle fingertips, stir vigorously until combined, adding more flour or warm water if needed to make a dough

What are the differences among kosher salt, sea salt and table salt?

According to food columnist Anne Garber, all salts are sodium chloride and therefore substantively identical. However, they are manufactured in different ways, which can result in different textures. Sea salt is made by evaporating trapped seawater and is sometimes preferred by people who believe that there are additional trace minerals in regular table salt. However, Garber quotes experts who explain that almost all trace materials are processed out of sea salt and that it is nearly identical to regular table salt.

Kosher salt and table salt are manufactured in similar fashion, with water being forced into a salt deposit, leaving brine that dries. However, kosher salt is raked during the process, which gives it a lighter and flakier texture. Many cooks prefer using kosher salt because it seems a bit less "salty." Finally, iodine is sometimes added to table salt (to prevent goiter), but kosher salt has no additives, another reason some cooks may prefer this salt.

POTATO-ONION BREAD
(CONTINUED)

that comes together. Turn out onto a flat surface and knead 7 or 8 minutes, until the dough is smooth and somewhat elastic.

Transfer to a lightly oiled shallow container (such as a pie plate), cover loosely with a plastic bag (like the kind groceries are packed in) or plastic wrap, and let rise in a warm place (75 to 80 degrees F) such as a gas oven with a pilot light, until double in volume, about 2 hours. Place on lightly floured surface and knead 2 to 3 minutes. Transfer back to shallow container and cover with plastic bag. Return to warm place and let rise until double in volume, about 2 hours. Remove from shallow container and form into a round loaf approximately 10 inches in diameter and 2 inches high. Place on pizza stone or heavy cookie sheet. Cover loosely with plastic bag and let rise in a warm place until almost double in size, about 1 hour.

Preheat oven to 375 degrees F. Sprinkle bread with coarse kosher salt and, using a sharp knife, make several cross-hatch slashes about ¼-inch deep into the top of the dough. Bake approximately 1 hour, or until bread is uniformly browned and the bottom sounds hollow when tapped with your knuckle. Remove from oven and let cool to room temperature. May be sliced and warmed in the oven before serving.

MIXED GREENS WITH APPLES AND BLUE CHEESE

Look for crisp, tart apples and mild blue cheese for this elegant salad. If you're serving six or eight people, double the recipe.
Makes about 4 servings.

10 ounces mixed greens, washed and dried

1 large apple, halved, cored, and thinly sliced

¼ cup olive oil

2½ tablespoons white wine vinegar

Salt and pepper, to taste

3 ounces blue cheese, crumbled

In a large bowl, combine the greens and apple. In a small bowl, whisk together the olive oil and vinegar to form a smooth emulsion. Drizzle over the greens, season with salt and pepper; toss well. Arrange on individual plates and garnish with the blue cheese. Serve immediately.

Never eat more than you can lift.

Miss Piggy

The back door is sticking...

My best friend decided to give me the ultimate housewarming present: She basically fixed all the little things about my new house that I hated. I had to move to a new city and had sold the house I loved, moving to a new one I really didn't like as much. Knowing I was depressed about moving in, she borrowed the key, came over before I moved, and went to work. The kitchen cabinets were sticky and disgusting from years of other occupants—she scoured them with strong chemicals so that they were completely clean. I hated the cheap front door—she bought me a new one, which she wrapped in a big red bow. She caulked the bathroom floor, spackled, sanded and, best of all, painted the drab kitchen a bright sunny yellow. She eventually drafted her boyfriend, neighbors, and me onto her work crew, and set us all to work on fixing up the entire house. Sure, she could have thrown some big housewarming party where I received a bunch of gifts I already owned. But fixing up my house so that I could move into it was the ultimate gift. When the work was done, we all sat around in our paint-covered clothes, opened a bottle of champagne, and celebrated the fact that my new home was ready for me. I'll always be grateful for her thoughtfulness and hard work. (Oh, and if she's reading this—the back door is sticking a bit, can you get right on it?)

Josie

A Perfect Party Favor

To help your friends feel a part of your new home, we suggest giving them a piece of it, such as:

* If your new home has property around it, collect small stones from your backyard and paint a phrase or word on each one with water-based acrylic paint—phrases such as "enduring friendship" or "girlfriends forever." You could also paint a word that best describes each friend, such as "courageous," "inspirational," or "awesome."

* Get a Polaroid® camera with enough film so that everyone can take a picture home with them. Take group pictures outside by a newly planted tree, an ugly kitchen, or some other landmark that you plan on changing over time. Write the date on each picture with the promise that you'll all get together again and see how the new house has become a home.

HEARTY SMOKED HAM SOUP WITH LIMA BEANS

Homemade chicken stock is always best to use when making soup, but if you can't spare the time to make a pot, use commercial chicken broth sold in boxes or small cartons in the soup section of the grocery store.

Makes 8 to 10 servings.

5 tablespoons unsalted butter

¾ cup all-purpose flour

5½ quarts homemade chicken stock or low-sodium chicken broth

1 teaspoon each sage leaves and thyme

1 large onion, cut into dice, ¼ to ½"

2 large carrots, cut into dice, ¼ to ½"

2 10-ounce packages frozen lima beans, thawed

1½ pounds lean smoked ham, cut into small dice

Salt and pepper, to taste

In a heavy-bottomed pot large enough to hold all the ingredients, melt the butter over moderate heat. Add the flour and mix well. Cook 5 minutes, stirring frequently, until the mixture is golden brown and slightly sandy in texture. Slowly add about 1 cup of the chicken broth, stirring constantly with a wire whisk to form a smooth emulsion free of lumps. Slowly add about 2 more cups, whisking constantly until thoroughly com-

An easy recipe for homemade chicken broth...

Our friend Linda is a natural host: She enjoys cooking and entertaining and does both with a carefree, joyful attitude some of the most accomplished hosts cannot achieve. She is a "comfortable cook," often developing her own recipes and modifying others. We asked her to share her easy chicken broth recipe with us. She recommends using a leftover chicken carcass (or if you have not served chicken lately, ask the butcher for several pounds of backs and necks). Put the bones and anything still on it, including the skin, in a large pot with water just covering the bones. Add a chopped-up onion, an unpeeled carrot, and some salt (not much) and pepper. You may also add a bay leaf or other herbs if you like. Bring to a boil and then turn the heat down so that it simmers for several hours. Strain and refrigerate until all the fat rises to the top, which can then be easily lifted off. The stock can be frozen or used right away.

Family Recipe Night

Our friend Susan told us about the lovely way her closest friends helped settle her into her new home. She had invited them to a housewarming dinner, and unknown to her, the group of friends got together ahead of time and decided to bring her the favorite recipes from their respective families. They also chipped in to purchase a sweet little box to hold the recipes and the pans needed to prepare them. The instigator of this wonderful idea, Beverly, told Susan it was what her mother had done for her when she moved into her first home, providing instruction on how to make many of the dishes her mother, aunt, and grandmother had made for Beverly throughout her life. Susan told us that, to this day, those recipes and kitchen items from her friends are among her most cherished possessions.

SMOKED HAM SOUP
(CONTINUED)

bined. Add the remaining chicken stock, along with the sage, thyme, and onion. Bring to a boil over high heat. Reduce the heat to moderate and simmer 30 minutes, stirring frequently and scraping the bottom of the pan for the first 10 minutes, and occasionally thereafter.

Add the carrots, lima beans, and ham and cook 20 to 25 minutes, or until the carrots and lima beans are just tender. Season with salt and pepper and serve immediately. Will keep in a tightly sealed container in the refrigerator for up to 5 days.

Cooking is like love. It should be entered into with abandon or not at all.

Harriet Van Horne
Vogue (October 1956)

CARROT CAKE WITH CREAM CHEESE FROSTING

Some folks prefer a simpler rendition of this classic, but if you like carrot cake with added sweetness and texture, include the suggested raisins and/or walnuts to the batter.
Makes about 15 servings.

Cake:

1 cup vegetable oil

1¼ cups granulated sugar

3 eggs

2¼ cups all-purpose flour

1 tablespoon baking powder

2 teaspoons baking soda

1½ tablespoons cinnamon

3 cups finely grated carrots, squeezed of excess juice

1 cup coarsely chopped walnuts or golden raisins

Cream Cheese Frosting:

6 ounces cream cheese, softened

2 tablespoons unsalted butter

3 cups confectioners' sugar, sifted to remove lumps

2 teaspoons vanilla extract

A Gardenwarming

I once went to a "gardenwarming" party at a girlfriend's house to celebrate her new home. She had purchased a lovely home, but the garden was a mess. Before the gardenwarming, she paid a gardener to pull out existing weeds and overgrown flowers, and leave fresh dirt and garden beds. She then put dirt-filled pots all around the patio. We all showed up with wine, food, and plants. I brought two huge lavender plants, which we put in pots on each side of her back door. Another friend brought several herb plants, which we planted close together and then encircled with flowers, creating an herb and cutting garden. Someone remembered the cat, bringing fresh catnip and cat mint plants and planting them at the base of a cement cat statue they also brought. In just a couple of hours, the garden was completely transformed, and everyone enjoyed sitting outside in their gardening clothes and mud-covered shoes sipping wine.

Denise

A Decorating Tip

In the same way that color-coordinated decorations show you put extra effort into making an event memorable, the lighting also affects the mood and the memories.

* Few people look their best under fluorescent lights. If possible, replace them with soft-glow light bulbs. If that's not possible, then turn them off and rely on other forms of lighting.

* Everyone does look her best by candlelight. Consider turning off electric lights completely and entertaining solely by the light of candles and oil lamps. Just be careful to set the candles away from draperies and in holders that can collect wax and do not tip easily.

* You'll love the atmosphere created by draping rose-colored scarves over lampshades. Use a low-wattage bulb and make sure the fabric is not touching the bulb or getting too hot.

* For a different twist in lighting, fill large glass vases with Christmas lights, either colored or all-white, and place them around the room for pleasant ambient lighting.

CARROT CAKE
(CONTINUED)

For the cake: Preheat oven to 350 degrees F. Generously grease a 9-by-13-inch baking pan. In a large bowl, using an electric mixer, beat together the oil and sugar until thoroughly combined. Add 1 egg at a time, beating well between additions, until the mixture is smooth and pale in color. Add the flour, baking powder, baking soda, and cinnamon and mix well. Stir in the carrots, and raisins and walnuts if desired, and mix well. Pour into prepared pan. Bake on bottom shelf approximately 30 minutes. Transfer to upper shelf and bake 10 additional minutes, or until top is golden brown and toothpick inserted into the center comes out clean. Cool to room temperature on baking rack.

To make the frosting: In a medium bowl, using an electric mixer, beat the cream cheese and butter until soft. Add the confectioners' sugar and beat until thoroughly combined and smooth. Add the vanilla extract and mix well. Store in the refrigerator for at least 1 hour before using. Spread the frosting over the top of the cake. Cut into serving squares and serve at room temperature. Cake will keep at cool room temperature covered with plastic wrap for 3 to 4 days.

For Guests at a Housewarming

We often bring a gift to a girlfriend when visiting her for the first time in her new home—flowers, wine, a candle, a gift that helps celebrate this new beginning and makes a house more personal to her. Remember Donna Reed, who in her role as Mary Bailey in *It's a Wonderful Life*, brought gifts to a family celebrating a new home? She brought bread, symbolizing her wish that no one in that house would ever experience hunger; salt, so that their lives would always have flavor; and wine, symbolizing her desire that the occupants would experience joy and prosperity. When we want to specify our hopes for a friend in a new home, we may want to fill a basket full with items symbolizing those hopes, along with a note that expresses what meaning each item brings. Alternatively, we may want to organize a house blessing ceremony using some of those items. We have adapted this ceremony from the book *Where the Heart Is* to help you articulate your best wishes for your girlfriend:

Bring with you a basket containing a feather, candle, salt, bread, and wine or sparkling apple juice. If it is just close girlfriends at the party, this ceremony may be performed any time. If a lot of people are invited, you may want to organize the closest girlfriends to come an hour early (letting your girlfriend know, of course!) and perform the ceremony before others arrive. When the appropriate time for the ceremony comes, gather together and say to your friend:

* For as long as you live here, your cares will be as light as this feather. Your worries will float gently out of the window and away. (Open the window and let the feather drift away in the breeze.)
* For as long as you live here, your path will be lit like the flame of this candle. Your home will shelter and protect you so the flame will burn ever bright and warm. (Light the candle.)
* For as long as you live here, your life will be full of flavor like this salt. (Present the salt to your friend.)
* For as long as you live here, your soul will be nourished, as we are nourished by this bread. You shall never hunger in body or spirit. (Break the bread so that everyone may enjoy a bite.)
* For as long as you live here, you will be surrounded by love and laughter and never feel lonely. (Pass a glass of wine or apple juice around so that everyone may take a sip.)
* We joyfully welcome you into your new home.

You may modify this ceremony as you like, either adding other wishes or saying a prayer blessing the home and your friend. Feel free to modify as you wish.

Memories

Include here memories of your housewarming: a picture of close friends, a "before" picture of a room you intend on changing, and your plans for your new home!

A Hallelujah Lunch

Can you believe it? You actually did it! After all this time and all that work! And would you have made it without the support and encouragement of your girlfriends? Probably not. This is your chance to bask in the spotlight, celebrate an achievement, and to thank your girlfriends for believing you could make it, even when you had some doubts. Share your winning moment with those who have traveled with you along the way. This is also a wonderful way to say "I'm so proud of you" to a friend who has faced a challenge and won.

Menu

KIR COCKTAILS*

MIXED GREENS WITH WALNUTS AND FENNEL*

ASPARAGUS AND GREEN BEANS WITH WARM TOMATO VINAIGRETTE*

SHRIMP BISQUE*

VANILLA-POACHED DRIED FIGS AND APRICOTS WITH FRESH CHEESE*

MIXED GREENS WITH WALNUTS AND FENNEL

For the mixed greens, select a combination of rocket, frisée, radicchio, endive, watercress, and baby lettuces, or any prepackaged medley, if preferred.

Makes 8 servings.

10 ounces mixed greens, washed and thoroughly dried

2 bulbs fennel, trimmed, cored, and thinly sliced

½ cup coarsely chopped toasted walnuts

6 tablespoons olive oil

2 tablespoons balsamic vinegar

2 cloves garlic, minced

Salt and pepper, to taste

In a large bowl, toss together the greens, fennel, and walnuts. In a small bowl, mix together the olive oil, balsamic vinegar, garlic, salt, and pepper using a wire whisk to form a smooth emulsion. Drizzle over the greens and toss well. Serve immediately.

Absolutely Fabulous

Start a "Hallelujah Journal" and write a short description of the accomplishment you are celebrating, with the date and the names of all in attendance. Let the current "winner" keep the book until the next time your group of girlfriends gathers to celebrate another success. After entering the new "winner's" name and accomplishment in the book, let her take custody of the journal until your next celebratory event. Later, when you read back over your gatherings, you'll be amazed at how wonderful and successful you and your girlfriends are!

A Pleasing Cocktail

* A Kir cocktail is a festive, beautifully colored cocktail befitting a celebratory occasion. And it is easy to make! Just pour up to ¾ ounce of crème de cassis into a wine glass, fill with white wine, and garnish with a lemon twist. If you wish to make the drink less sweet, decrease the amount of the cassis. For a Kir Royale, which is even more festive, use champagne or sparkling wine instead of the white wine.

Help is near!

Is there any of us who has not been faced with a crisis in the kitchen an hour before your guests are to arrive? Usually a call to our mother, sisters, friends, or favorite cooks will help solve the problem; but if they are not around and you have a computer and Web hookup, get on the Internet. For those who are already familiar with researching on the Web, you know that you can ask any question of general search engines and probably get the help you need. Many cooks we know swear by epicurious.com, a Web site focused exclusively on food and cooking, which provides instruction, directs you to recipes at other Web sites, and can help you find ingredients that may not be available at your local store. Try it—it is addictive!

ASPARAGUS AND GREEN BEANS WITH WARM TOMATO VINAIGRETTE

If pencil-thin asparagus are unavailable, use the thicker asparagus; slice each stalk lengthwise to make its thickness uniform with the green beans. Feel free to add more garlic if you're an avid lover of the stinking rose.
Makes 8 servings.

2 bunches pencil-thin asparagus, trimmed

10 ounces green beans, trimmed

3 tomatoes, finely chopped

4 cloves garlic, finely chopped

3 tablespoons olive oil

¼ teaspoon thyme

Salt and pepper, to taste

In a large pot, bring 6 quarts of water to boil over high heat. Add the asparagus and green beans and cook 2 to 3 minutes, or until crisp-tender. Drain in a colander and refresh with cold water. Immediately transfer to a bowl filled with ice water. When chilled throughout, drain well in colander. Transfer to a large platter.

Heat a medium sauté pan over high heat until it is hot but not smoking. Add the tomatoes, garlic, olive oil, and thyme and cook 2 minutes, stirring frequently. Season with salt and pepper and mix well. Pour over asparagus and green beans and serve immediately.

SHRIMP BISQUE

The best way to make a deeply flavored, rich seafood bisque is to use homemade seafood or fish stock. And the best way to make good seafood stock is by using shrimp shells saved and stored in the freezer for just this purpose. If you don't happen to have such a stash, ask your fish monger for fish bones and heads from mild-tasting white fish like halibut, snapper, and bass to substitute for the shrimp shells in the recipe below.

Makes 8 to 10 servings.

Shrimp stock:

14 cups loosely packed shrimp shells

1 onion, quartered

1 bunch parsley, including stems, coarsely chopped

10 whole black peppercorns

8 to 10 quarts water

Place the shrimp shells, onion, parsley, peppercorn, and 8 quarts of water in a 12-quart stockpot. Bring to a boil over high heat, taking care not to let it boil over. Reduce the heat to moderate and simmer 2½ to 3 hours, stirring frequently and pushing the shells back into the boiling water (they tend to rise to the surface and remain there). Keep the water level even by adding additional water to the stock as it cooks away. Remove from heat and cool to room temperature. Strain through a fine wire mesh and discard the shells (or fish bones). There should be about 5 quarts of strained stock.

Fleeting Fame

One of my friends, Jean, was convinced I was not doing enough to commemorate my first book being published. In celebration, Jean threw a party for me at our favorite local restaurant, invited all our friends and current and former coworkers, and, unbeknownst to me, called the society page editor of our local paper to "report" the party. Much to our surprise (as we live in a city with many well-known authors), the party was the first item in the column the next day! What an unexpected gift!

Pamela

On Invitations

For informal events, it is perfectly accept-able to telephone your invitations. You can add a new twist, however, by sending an invitation by other means and in other forms.

* E-viting: Send out your invitations via evite.com. Everyone will see who's invited and be all the more excited about attending. Encourage your guests to e-mail before the day of the event.

* Put invitations on thick grade cardboard and cut them into jigsaw puzzles.

* For computer literates (or even semi-literates), get a card making program and personalize your invitation. If you have a scanner, you can even include a picture of yourself, of the group or anything else you wish to show off.

* An invitation no-no: Don't put sparkly, sticky stuff in the invitation that falls all over the floor, into the dog food, and attaches permanently to the recipient's wool sweater.

SHRIMP BISQUE
(CONTINUED)

Bisque:

5 tablespoons unsalted butter

⅓ cup all-purpose flour

4 quarts shrimp stock

16 ounces tomato paste

½ pint heavy cream

¼ cup dry sherry

Salt and pepper, to taste

1 pound bay shrimp

In a large, heavy-bottomed pot, melt the butter over moderately low heat until melted. Add the flour and cook, stirring frequently, 3 to 4 minutes, or until it is a pale golden brown. Slowly add the shrimp stock, whisking con-stantly to make a smooth mixture and to pre-vent lumps from forming. Continue adding stock, whisking constantly, until it is all added. Bring to a boil over high heat, stirring constantly, alternating with a wooden spoon (to scrape the bottom of the pot) and the whisk (to keep lumps from forming). Add the tomato paste and cream and mix well. Reduce the heat to moderate and simmer 30 to 35 minutes, or until the soup is the consistency of heavy cream. Add the sherry and season with salt and pep-per to taste. Just before serving, add the shrimp and mix well.

VANILLA-POACHED DRIED FIGS AND APRICOTS WITH FRESH CHEESE

This lovely dessert makes a lasting impression on family and friends—don't tell them how easy it is to make! When selecting vanilla pods, look for fat, shiny, pliable pods that feel greasy to the touch.

Makes 8 servings.

1 vanilla pod

1 1.5 liter white wine (7 cups)

2½ cups water

2 tablespoons dried orange peel

1⅓ cups granulated sugar

1 pound dried Mission figs, stemmed

8 ounces dried apricots

1 15-ounce container low-fat ricotta cheese

⅓ cup sifted confectioners' sugar

Dash nutmeg

Sprigs of mint, for garnish

Use a paring knife to split the vanilla pod lengthwise. Scrape the seeds from inside the pod and place in a heavy-bottomed pot. Add the split vanilla pod, wine, water, orange peel, and sugar. Bring to a boil over high heat. Reduce the heat to moderate and simmer 1 hour, stirring occasionally. Add the figs and cook 30 minutes, stirring occasionally. Add the apricots and cook an additional 15 minutes, or

About Vanilla

Vanilla pods, or beans, are generally available in natural food stores, or specialty or gourmet grocery stores, although they aren't cheap—we visited one store where a small glass vial cost twelve dollars! Put in historical perspective, however, vanilla pods seem reasonably priced. As Diane Ackerman tells us in her delicious *Anatomy of the Senses*, by the 1500s, vanilla was "prized so highly that Montezuma drank an infusion of it as a royal balm and demanded vanilla beans in tribute from his subjects. . . Cortes valued vanilla enough to carry bags of it back to Europe, along with the Aztecs' gold, silver, jewels and chocolate. A passion for vanilla, especially in combination with chocolate, raged in Europe, where it was prized as an aphrodisiac." So perhaps buying authentic vanilla is a case of "you get what you pay for," especially when compared with artificial vanilla, comprised of synthetic vanillin, which is produced from the by-products of paper manufacturing!

Cooking Tip

* Can I use any kind of fig in this dessert?

Use any dried figs, but Mission is best because it provides a contrasting color to the apricots.

POACHED FIGS
(CONTINUED)

until the fruit is plump and soft. Remove from the heat and cool to room temperature. Remove the vanilla pod and discard.

In a medium bowl, combine the ricotta cheese, confectioners' sugar, and nutmeg; mix well.

To serve: Place a dollop of cheese in a shallow bowl and add some fruit. Drizzle with some of the poaching liquid and garnish with a sprig of mint.

Memories

Start your Hallelujah Journal here or add a photo of an event you have celebrated with friends.

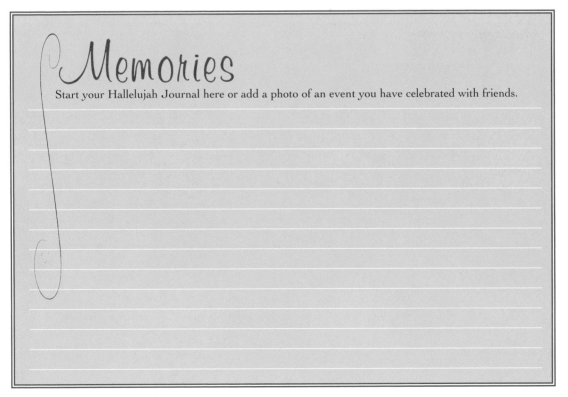

Memories and Notes

Photos

Counting on Each Other

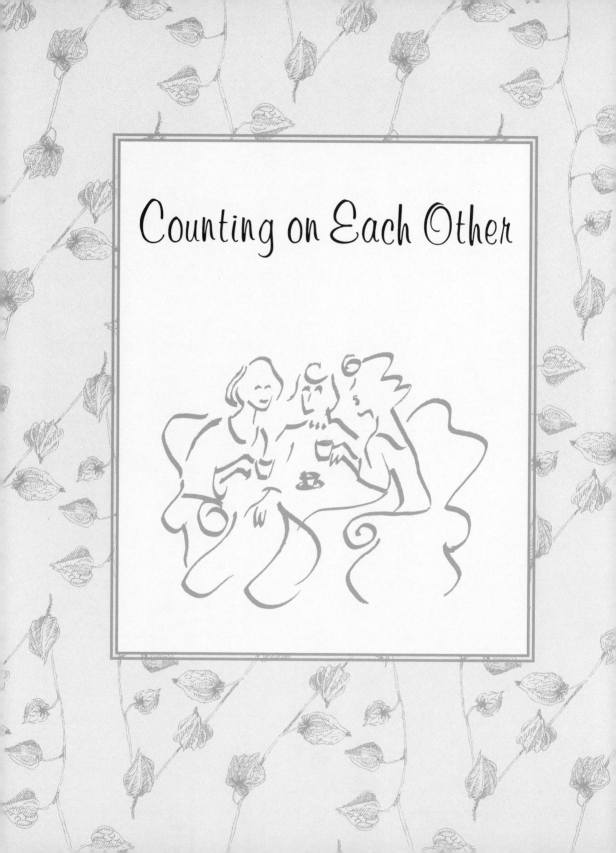

Chapters

You're Better Off without Him Supper

Take Comfort Dinner

Safety Net Social

You're Better Off without Him Supper

Who needs him? You don't. Who wants him? Not you. Who misses him? Well, you might just a little, so now is the time to gather your girlfriends to remind you about all of his faults, failings, and foibles. You're better off without him. Really.

Menu

WINE OR COCKTAILS

FRIED CHICKEN*

MASHED POTATOES WITH SWEET BUTTER*

CREAMED CORN OR FRESH GREEN BEANS

WHITE CHOCOLATE BROWNIES*

CHOCOLATE–CHOCOLATE CHIP ICE CREAM
WITH MILK CHOCOLATE SAUCE

SEE'S CANDIES® OR OTHER BOXED CANDY ASSORTMENT

FRIED CHICKEN

It's best to use a cooking thermometer when frying chicken unless you're very experienced with cooking in hot oil. While the temperature will vary depending on the size of the chicken and how many pieces are cooking at one time, it's best to stay between 315 and 325 degrees F when cooking chicken parts. You may keep the breasts and wings warm in a very low oven while cooking the remaining chicken, but food cooked in this fashion retains heat for a long time.

Makes 2 to 4 servings.

4 pounds whole chicken, cut up
   (2 breasts, 2 drumsticks, 2 thighs,
   and 2 wings)

1½ cups buttermilk

2 cups all-purpose flour

¼ cup cornmeal

2½ teaspoons kosher salt

1 teaspoon black pepper

1½ to 2 quarts canola oil

Place chicken and buttermilk in large bowl and cover tightly. Refrigerate overnight or for 24 hours, turning chicken pieces occasionally. Remove from refrigerator 1 hour before cooking. In a large, shallow bowl, combine the flour, cornmeal, salt, and pepper. Remove the breasts and wings from the buttermilk and add to the dry ingredients. Coat all sides evenly with the flour mixture.

Using Cooking Thermometers

This recipe calls for measuring the temperature of the oil in which the chicken cooks, for which you use a deep-fry thermometer, as opposed to a meat thermometer. When measuring the temperature of oil, the tip of the thermometer should be two inches into the oil to get an accurate reading.

If you are measuring the temperature of the meat itself, such as when roasting a chicken or ham, you would use a meat thermometer, of which there are two types: an ovenproof one, which should be inserted in the meat before cooking, where it remains until the meat is done; and an "instant" thermometer, inserted in the meat to take its temperature in a few seconds (much like taking your own temperature). The instant

thermometer is not left in the meat during roasting time. When using either meat thermometer, make sure that it is inserted a couple of inches into the thickest part of the meat and away from fat, gristle, and bone.

While most meat thermometers will come with instructions as to recommended cooking times, oven temperatures, and internal temperatures for various meats, you can also learn this and other information about the safe cooking of meat through the USDA's Meat and Poultry Hotline at 1-800-535-4555 or at www.foodsafety.gov.

See's Candies®

* If you live on the West Coast, you already know about See's Candies® and how delectable they are. If you would like to try them yourself, you can order them by calling 1-800-915-7337 or going to their website at sees.com.

FRIED CHICKEN (CONTINUED)

In a very large skillet (at least 12 inches), heat 1½ quarts of oil over moderately high heat to 325 degrees F. Add the breasts and wings and cook, turning occasionally and maintaining the heat, for 15 to 17 minutes. Drain on paper towels. Reduce the temperature of the oil to 315 degrees F. Place the thighs and drumsticks in the flour mixture and coat all sides evenly. Add to the oil and cook, turning occasionally, 15 to 17 minutes for the drumsticks and 22 to 24 minutes for the thighs. Cooking time will depend on the consistency and temperature of the oil and the size of the chicken pieces. Drain on paper towels and serve immediately.

A salad is not a meal. It is a style.

Fran Lebowitz,
Metropolitan Life (1978)

MASHED POTATOES WITH SWEET BUTTER

Everyone has a favorite way to make mashed potatoes; this is our version. We prefer nonfat, rather than whole, milk as the moistening agent because the milder taste enhances, rather than masks, the flavor of the potatoes. Yukon Gold potatoes have the most pronounced flavor and the best texture for this classic dish, but if they are unavailable, substitute white or red new potatoes.

6 medium-large Yukon Gold potatoes, peeled and cut into 1½-inch pieces

2 to 4 tablespoons unsalted butter

¾ to 1 cup nonfat milk

Kosher salt and white pepper, to taste

Place potatoes in a large pot and cover with cold water. Bring to a boil over high heat. Reduce the heat to moderate and cook 12 to 15 minutes, or until the potatoes are tender when pierced with a sharp knife. Drain well in a colander. Meanwhile, rinse out the cooking pot with fresh water. Return to the stove, add the butter, and melt over low heat. Return the potatoes to the pot along with the milk and, using a hand-masher, mash the potatoes until they are nearly smooth. Season with salt and pepper and serve immediately, accompanied by a small bowl of unsalted butter softened to room temperature.

Some Pick-Me-Up Techniques

Everyone who has experienced a breakup knows that a woman's self-confidence is often shaken by it, no matter who officially ended the relationship. When you are hosting a "You're Better Off without Him Supper," help your girlfriend get back on her "I'm a lovable and sexy babe!" feet again by:

* Treating her to a manicure and pedicure before she comes over for the dinner so she'll feel like a queen from the get-go.

* Create a list of other gorgeous women in her age range who have recently entered into new relationships or a list of gorgeous women she will always be younger than.

* Ask each guest to name one thing that your girlfriend will be free to do now that she is no longer with her ex.

* Use part of your time together to plan a weekend trip or day-long adventure in the near future.

Why let a good ring go to waste?

My business partner and I have the same name, Lynn. We're a lot alike in many ways. One day we were at her place and we started swapping stories about our exes and some of the items they bought us during courtship. We soon found out that each of us had been given a gold ring with blue sapphires and diamonds. I told her I no longer wanted to wear any of the jewelry this man had given me. She expressed the same feeling about her ring. Then the light bulb went off. I said, "Even though it is a beautiful ring, I don't want to wear it anymore so I am going to give it to you." She laughed and said, "Wait a minute. Follow me." We walked back into her bedroom where she pulled out her ring and gave it to me. She and I both like the new rings better than the ones we had, and can each enjoy with the sweet memory of a dear girlfriend instead of the heartache of a man who didn't deserve us!

Lynn

What a great idea!

* If you and your girlfriends have gifts from former mates that you no longer enjoy, but hate to see unused, bring them all together for a particular kind of swap meet—one that clears out painful reminders while bringing healing and pleasure to everyone involved. What could be better?

WHITE CHOCOLATE BROWNIES

This luscious confection is a cross between brownies and a very rich cake. The brownies will keep at a cool room temperature, tightly sealed in plastic wrap, for up to 4 days. Makes 6 to 8 servings.

6 tablespoons unsalted butter, softened to room temperature

1 cup sugar

2 eggs

1 tablespoon vanilla extract

1 cup nonfat vanilla yogurt

4 ounces white chocolate, melted and slightly cooled

1½ cups all-purpose flour

2½ teaspoons baking powder

½ teaspoon baking soda

Preheat oven to 350 degrees F. Generously grease an 8-by-8-inch baking pan.

In a medium bowl, using an electric mixer, beat together the butter and sugar for 3 minutes. Add the eggs and vanilla and beat 2 minutes. Mix in the yogurt and white chocolate. Sprinkle over the top the flour, baking powder, and baking soda. Beat 1 minute, or until thoroughly mixed. Pour into prepared pan. Bake on bottom shelf of oven 37 to 40 minutes, or

How to melt chocolate

If you have ever ended up with a pile of bitter, "seized up" chocolate, you understand the difficulty in doing what seems to happen so easily in the bottom of your purse or in your glove compartment. Melting chocolate is actually a bit of a tricky business. The keys to success are frequent stirring and not letting the chocolate come into direct contact with the source of the heat. When melting chocolate on top of the stove, most cooks recommend chopping the chocolate into small pieces with a bread or other serrated knife and putting it into a "double boiler," which is a pot within a pot. Heat water in the bottom of the "outside" pot until it is just simmering, and the steam heats the chocolate, which is in the "inside" pot. You can actually buy a doubleboiler for this purpose, but you can also improvise by using a heat-safe bowl that is big enough to sit on the rim of the outside pot without coming into contact with the simmering water. This is one pot you should definitely watch: When you see the chocolate just starting to melt, take the bowl off the water and stir the chocolate, then put it back on the simmering water.

Repeat this process until the chocolate is melted. If you instead want to use your microwave, cut up the chocolate and melt it at a high setting on the microwave, removing the chocolate every fifteen seconds or so (depending on the microwave) to stir it, repeating until the chocolate is melted.

As with most fine things, chocolate has its seasons. There is a simple memory aid that you can use to determine whether it is the correct time to order chocolate dishes: Any month whose name contains the letter a, e, or u is the proper time for chocolate.

Sandra Boynton
Chocolate: The Consuming Passion (1982)

WHITE CHOCOLATE BROWNIES (CONTINUED)

until a toothpick inserted into the outside edge of the brownies comes out clean. The center will be slightly sunken-in. Cool on baking rack. To serve, cut into squares.

Why does chocolate help a broken heart anyway?

Copious research has been conducted to understand our craving for chocolate when we are emotionally down. So far, medical science says chocolate doesn't have enough good stuff in it (or any more than any other food) to make a difference to a broken heart. Medical science obviously has not progressed far enough, however, because anyone whose heart has been broken knows better! It may be theobromine, it may be endorphins, it may be the psychological satisfaction of having a guilty pleasure instantly satisfied; but whatever it is, chocolate—whether in the form of bonbons, brownies, or ice cream or served hot in milk—can cure a broken heart (at least for a while). Who cares why—whatever the reason, it's real!

Take Comfort Dinner

When the ground falls out from beneath us, our girlfriends are there to catch us, with understanding, support, and a casserole or two. When we see a girlfriend dealing with a crisis, we are willing to jump in to help any way we can, but sometimes all we may be able to do is be with her and make sure she eats something.

Menu

CHOPPED ROMAINE SALAD WITH CREAMY DRESSING AND CROUTONS*

MACARONI AND CHEESE WITH BROCCOLI AND HAM*

GARLIC BREAD*

BUTTERSCOTCH-PECAN BLONDIES*

CHOPPED ROMAINE SALAD WITH CREAMY DRESSING AND CROUTONS

The best way to prepare the lettuce for this salad begins with trimming 1 inch from the tip of the lettuce and discarding. Next, slice each bunch in half lengthwise to the core; then slice the halves lengthwise to the core. Cut across into 1-inch pieces and discard the core.

2 bunches romaine lettuce, trimmed and cut into 1-inch pieces

¼ cup low-fat mayonnaise

¼ cup lemon juice

3 tablespoons anchovy paste

2 tablespoons vegetable oil

1 tablespoon prepared mustard

2 cloves garlic, minced

1 to 2 tablespoons cold water

6 ounces salad croutons

Place the lettuce in a large bowl. In a small bowl, whisk together the mayonnaise, lemon juice, and anchovy paste. Slowly add the oil, whisking constantly to form a smooth emulsion. Stir in the mustard, garlic, and 1 tablespoon of water or enough to make it the consistency of salad dressing. Drizzle over the lettuce and add the croutons; toss gently and serve immediately.

A Healing Weekend

To help me recover from my second cancer surgery, my soulmate friend flew from Arizona to spend two months in Ohio with me. We, along with two other close friends who lived near me, and my daughter, headed up to a Victorian summer lake town. What we didn't expect was an early winter and this, I must emphasize, was a summer resort. Picture the five of us bundled in winter coats, hoods up, scarves over our mouths, mittens, and boots—inside! Our breath showed frosty in the air. Our laughter hung and echoed in the quiet cold. We had snowball fights, made angels in the fresh snow, skated on the frozen lake with the lighthouse as our lifeguard, and drank hot chocolate with a splurge of whipped cream on top. At night we played silly word games that has us laughing so hard we all had tears running down our cheeks. Each of us agrees that was one of the best weekends of our lives.

Sue

That's something I've noticed about food: whenever there's a crisis if you get people to eating normally things get better.

Madeleine L'Engle
The Moon by Night (1963)

Giving Comfort

When personal crisis hits—one of our loved ones is gravely ill, we receive notice of being laid off, we lose a treasured pet—we can walk around in a stupor for a period of time. If a girlfriend is going through a trauma or tragedy, she needs her friends to be sensitive to the unique way she copes with grief and loss. Gather friends around to comfort her. But be careful not to force her to act the way you might under similar circumstances.

Remember:

* Some people may want their friends around, but not be asked to talk. Let her know you love her by your presence and by taking the spotlight off of her for a while.

* Other women need to talk about every detail. Give her the opportunity to tell you her story over and over and over again. Grief is often expressed, and relieved, through storytelling.

When you're all together as a group, organize a way each of you can help your friend, such as bringing over dinner each night for a week, running errands, searching the Internet for needed information, or simply checking in each day by phone.

MACARONI AND CHEESE WITH BROCCOLI AND HAM

Well-aged cheese, such as Canadian Cheddar, has a deep, nutty flavor that stands up to the assertive flavors of broccoli and smoky ham. If you can't find imported cheese for this dish, use very sharp domestic Cheddar instead. Makes about 6 servings.

1 pound elbow macaroni

1½ cups ½-inch broccoli flowerettes

3 tablespoons unsalted butter

5 tablespoons all-purpose flour

1 quart low-fat milk

2 tablespoons Dijon mustard

2 teaspoons paprika

¼ cup dry sherry

1 pound aged Canadian Cheddar cheese, grated

8 ounces smoked ham, cut into ½-inch chunks

Salt and pepper, to taste

Preheat oven to 350 degrees F. Lightly grease a 10-by-15-inch baking dish.

Cook macaroni according to package directions, less 5 minutes. During the last minute of cooking, add the broccoli, stir well, and cook

Truly comforting garlic bread

Instead of the sliced, buttered, and garlic-powdered bread that we nonchalantly throw in the oven, try this method for making garlic bread. While it may seem that the garlic taste will be too strong, the roasted garlic flavor is actually very subtle.

Peel most of the outside layers from a head of garlic and, using a serrated knife, cut the top of the garlic head off so that you can just see the tops of the raw garlic cloves. Drizzle a bit of olive oil over the top, put it into a covered pan or wrapped in aluminum foil (there are handy little earthenware bake dishes available for this purpose as well), and put into the oven at 425 degrees F. Bake for about forty-five minutes to an hour.

When cooled, serve with warm, crusty bread and sweet butter. Each clove can be pulled off the garlic head and squeezed onto the buttered, warm bread. Delicious!

Tomatoes and oregano make it Italian; wine and tarragon make it French. Sour cream makes it Russian; lemon and cinnamon make it Greek. Soy sauce makes it Chinese; garlic makes it good.

Alice May Brock
Alice's Restaurant Cookbook (1969)

MACARONI AND CHEESE (CONTINUED)

1 minute. Immediately remove from heat and drain the pasta and broccoli in a colander. Transfer to prepared pan and cover loosely with a damp kitchen towel. Set aside until needed.

In a heavy-bottomed pot, melt the butter over low heat. Add flour and cook 4 to 5 minutes, stirring frequently, until pale golden brown. Using a wire whisk, slowly add the milk, whisking constantly to prevent lumps from forming. Add the mustard and paprika and bring to a boil over high heat, whisking constantly and frequently scraping the bottom of the pan with a wooden spoon to keep the mixture from sticking and burning. Reduce the heat to moderately low and simmer 10 minutes, stirring occasionally. Add the sherry and cheese and stir until cheese melts. Add to the macaroni and broccoli, along with the ham. Mix well and season with salt and pepper.

Bake on lower shelf of oven 25 minutes, rotate to upper shelf, and bake an additional 10 minutes, or until mixture is light golden brown on top and bubbling hot. Remove from oven and let stand 5 minutes before serving.

BUTTERSCOTCH-PECAN BLONDIES

Here is a moist, rich brownie ideal for folks who aren't fond of chocolate—or who adore the toasty flavor of pecans and butterscotch. Makes about 12 servings.

8 tablespoons unsalted butter, softened to room temperature

6 tablespoons margarine, softened to room temperature

1½ cups light brown sugar

2 eggs

2½ teaspoons vanilla extract

1½ cups all-purpose flour

2 teaspoons baking powder

½ teaspoon baking soda

1 cup old-fashioned rolled oats

1 cup coarsely chopped toasted pecans

1 cup butterscotch chips

½ cup shredded coconut

Preheat oven to 350 degrees F. Generously grease a 9-by-13-inch baking pan.

In a large bowl, using an electric mixer, beat together the butter, margarine, and sugar for 3 minutes. Add the eggs and vanilla extract and beat 2 minutes. Sprinkle over the top the flour, baking powder, and baking soda and beat 1

My Guardian Angel

My good friend Elizabeth became my guardian angel during my mother's eight-month-long illness. My friends and family lived in Northern California, whereas I was the nursing mother of an infant and a four-year-old in Los Angeles. Depleting our savings account, I managed to fly up north three times to essentially say good-bye to Mom. Each visit, Elizabeth's husband met me at the airport, her own mother babysat while I was at the hospital, the entire family offered shoulders to cry on, and nobody ever complained about the inconvenience. Because of the selflessness of these friends, I was able to be at my mother's bedside when she died. I'll always be grateful.

Ellen

Food is the most primitive form of comfort.

Sheilah Graham
A State of Heat (1972)

BUTTERSCOTCH-PECAN BLONDIES
(CONTINUED)

minute. Stir in the oats, pecans, butterscotch chips, and coconut and mix well. Pour into prepared pan and bake in center of oven 30 to 35 minutes, or until the top is golden brown and a toothpick inserted into the center comes out clean.

Memories

What have been your favorite comfort foods? Include a recipe for one of them here.

Safety Net Social

Our long-term girlfriends form our safety net, the ones who know our histories, our secrets, our travails, and our successes. We check in with these friends to catch each other up on the events in our lives, and to give and receive reactions to them. Often these "check-ins" become a tradition—a monthly breakfast or dinner or an annual retreat that we know will leave us feeling a little more balanced (and perhaps a little more full). Try out this menu, developed to accommodate hours of lingering around the table.

Menu

MILD AND BITTER GREEN SALAD WITH SUN-DRIED TOMATO
VINAIGRETTE*

PASTA SHELLS WITH RED BELL PEPPER, ITALIAN SAUSAGE,
AND BROCCOLI*

WARM BREAD WITH BALSAMIC VINEGAR AND OLIVE OIL

ASSORTED OLIVES AND CHEESES

TIRAMISU*

MILD AND BITTER GREEN SALAD WITH SUN-DRIED TOMATO VINAIGRETTE

Curly endive usually comes in fairly large bunches and is characterized by its long, spiky leaves. If you are unable to find this leafy green, substitute escarole instead. For added flavor and texture, add a few sliced raw mushrooms to this hearty salad.

Makes about 6 servings.

1 medium bunch curly endive, ends trimmed and cut into 1-inch pieces

2 small heads butter lettuce (or 1 bunch red or green leaf lettuce), cut into 1-inch pieces

⅓ cup minced (reconstituted) sun-dried tomatoes

¼ cup olive oil

2 tablespoons white wine vinegar

Place greens in a large bowl. In a small bowl, combine the sun-dried tomatoes with the oil and vinegar; mix well. Drizzle over the greens and toss gently. Serve immediately.

Do You Know?...

* reconstituted means soaked in water until filled with water and made plump and pliable.

No Secrets

Our true girlfriends see us at our best and worst, and most likely, they have seen our cooking at its best and worst! Every cook, no matter how experienced or talented, has had disasters in the kitchen, and they often form the basis of some of our fondest memories.

Christine recalls, "One New Year's Eve, I had an impromptu dinner party, and my friend Carol, a fearless cook, volunteered to bring dessert. We were enjoying ourselves immensely throughout dinner, and were made even happier by the sight of Carol's ice cream pie coming to the table. Not one of the ten of us noticed until we had sawed halfway through dessert, that she had forgotten to bake the crust before putting in the ice cream! We were having so much fun that none of us recognized that the crust was tough because it was raw!

"I was able to hold this story over her head until several years later, when she was dining at my house for Thanksgiving. Just before we sat down to dinner, I poured the too-hot gravy into a glass container that immediately cracked in half, triggering a twenty-minute debate on how we could safely salvage the gravy. Who can have Thanksgiving dinner without gravy? In the end, discretion won out over valor, we threw out the gravy and made some glass-free gravy with the small amount of turkey juice left in the pan. With a little gravy rationing and a lot of ribbing, we had a successful dinner. But Carol still loves to tease me about the time I tried to make her eat glass. After fifteen years of cooking for each other, among many "culinary successes," these are the food stories we are most fond of telling on one another."

The point? No one, other than the most boorish person, comes to your house for the food, but for your company, and the rest does not really matter. Besides, every cooking disaster can be obliterated with laughter, and who better to laugh with than your girlfriends?

Who makes up your safety net?

All over the world, groups of women meet at regular intervals to celebrate their lives and friendships with each other. Some groups have been meeting together for decades; others are just beginning to create their traditions. Since nothing bonds a group of girlfriends together like the traditions they maintain over the years, use some of your "check in" time with your closest friends to start some meaningful and fun-filled rituals such as:

* Create a scrap book, adding pictures of family or special events, jotting down poems group members have written or collected, describing adventures you've had together, setting goals or making wishes for the next time you meet.

* In between your times together, send around a chain letter in which each person adds an update to their lives and sends it on to another girlfriend in the circle. By the time you get together again, you'll feel like you've never been apart.

* Drop by a hardware store and select a color square in the paint department that most reminds you of each of your friends. At your next meeting, present each of them with her "color" with a short comment on what she means to you.

PASTA SHELLS WITH RED BELL PEPPER, ITALIAN SAUSAGE, AND BROCCOLI

Although this dish is full-flavored and very satisfying as is, feel free to serve with freshly grated Parmesan cheese. Substitute hot Italian sausage if you prefer a zippy flavor.
Makes 4 to 6 servings.

1¼ pounds mild Italian sausage, cut into
 ½-inch rounds

3 tablespoons olive oil

1 large red bell pepper, cut into ½-inch
 squares or triangles

4 cloves garlic, finely chopped

2 teaspoons each oregano and rosemary

1 pound large shell pasta

3 cups broccoli flowerettes

Salt and pepper, to taste

In a large sauté pan, cook the sausage in the olive oil over high heat 5 to 7 minutes, stirring frequently, until the sausage is browned on all sides. Reduce the heat to moderate and cook an additional 3 minutes, stirring frequently. Add the bell pepper, garlic, and herbs and cook 5 minutes, stirring occasionally, until the pepper is tender and sausage cooked through. Remove from the heat and set aside until needed.

The 1947 Girls

This special girlfriends group started fifty-three years ago, with the original four from the high school graduating class of 1947. Delores, Irene, Joyce, and Barbara started meeting for lunch once a month. As the years progressed, more girlfriends joined the group, and the latest count was twenty-five girlfriends. Every third Thursday of the month, the girlfriends meet for lunch at local restaurants.

Every July, they have a luncheon at Rita's beach house. A caravan of cars travels forty-five minutes to the shore, with everyone bringing a covered dish to enjoy as well as the recipe. A wonderful buffet, these meals are always special because they are made with love.

A get-well card is brought to the luncheon for anyone who cannot attend due to illness. Everyone signs the card and sends wishes for a quick recovery. In this way, each girlfriend is included in the annual celebration, even if it's only in thought.

Each get-together is full of laughter, stories, and memories, past and present. Even though some of these women were not especially close in high school, they now have a bond through shared experiences of life, marriage, children, jobs, retirement, grandchildren, and illnesses. They are looking forward to spending the next fifty-three years together.

The 1947 girls: Rita, Dolores, Doris, Marie, Mary, Florence, Barbara, Mary Lou, Joyce, Nancy, Joan, Miriam, Marie, Caroline, Elizabeth, Dorothy, Rose Mary, Margie, Sarah, Norma, Angie, Alice, Mary Jane, Jeanne, and Jackie.

Cheri

PASTA SHELLS (CONTINUED)

In a very large pot, bring 8 quarts of water to boil over high heat. Add the shells and cook 12 minutes, or until 2 minutes from being *al dente*. Add the broccoli, stir well, and cook 2 minutes, or until the broccoli is crisp-tender. Drain well in a colander, shaking to remove excess water. Transfer to a large bowl. Reheat the sausage mixture and add to the pasta. Season with salt and pepper and serve immediately.

Conversation's got to have some root in the past, or else you've got to explain every remark you make, an' it wears a person out.

Sarah Orne Jewett
The Country of the Pointed Firs (1896)

TIRAMISU

This dessert must be made and assembled one day before serving to allow the flavors to properly marry. If you're pressed for time, it's a good idea to make the Mexican Three Milk Cake the day before assembling the Tiramisu—it keeps very well covered with plastic wrap for one day.

Makes about 8 servings.

Mexican Three Milk Cake

5 egg whites

1¼ cups sugar

4 egg yolks

2 cups all-purpose flour

2½ teaspoons baking powder

¾ cup milk

2 teaspoons vanilla extract

Preheat oven to 350 degrees F. Generously grease a 13-by-9-inch baking pan.

Cooking Tip

* To make the quintessential Tiramisu, use the recipe for Mexican Three Milk Cake—a confection created especially for absorbing liquids. Some recipes call for ladyfingers or commercial sponge cake, but we find this version is best— even though it takes an extra step.

In a large bowl, using an electric mixer, beat the egg whites until stiff peaks form. Slowly add the sugar, beating constantly. Add the yolks one at a time, beating between each addition. Sprinkle the flour and baking powder over the top and mix well. Add the milk and vanilla extract and beat 2 minutes on high speed. Pour batter into prepared pan. Bake in center of oven approximately 20 minutes, or until the top is light golden brown and the center springs back when poked with a finger. Remove from oven and cool to room temperature on a baking rack. Just before preparing the Tiramisu, cut the cake into two 9 x 6-inch rectangles. Slice each rectangle in half through the center to make 4 thin layers.

Tiramisu

2 cups granulated sugar

1 cup strongly brewed dark
roast coffee

2 tablespoons dark rum

4 cups heavy cream

16 ounces mascarpone cheese

¼ cup confectioners' sugar

Dash nutmeg

4 ounces semisweet chocolate, very
finely chopped

2 tablespoons crème de cacao or white
chocolate liqueur

1 ounce milk chocolate, shaved, for
garnish

In a small saucepan, combine the sugar
and coffee. Cook over moderate heat
until boiling. Boil 1 minute and remove
from heat. Add the rum and mix well.
Cool in the freezer or refrigerator until
chilled and syrupy.

In a medium bowl, using an electric
mixer, beat one-half of the heavy cream
until stiff peaks form. Add the mascarpone cheese, confectioners' sugar, nut-

meg, and finely chopped chocolate; beat until
thoroughly mixed.

Assemble the Tiramisu

Place one layer of the cake on a large, flat plate
or serving platter. Using a pastry brush, dab
about ¼ of the coffee syrup over the surface,
taking care to evenly soak the cake. Gently
spread ⅓ of the mascarpone mixture over the
cake. Add a second cake layer. Dab with ¼ of
the coffee syrup and top with ⅓ of the mascarpone mixture. Add a third layer and dab with ¼
of the coffee syrup; spread the remaining mascarpone mixture over the top. Add the fourth
cake layer and dab with the remaining coffee
syrup. Wrap tightly in plastic and refrigerate
for 24 hours.

To serve the Tiramisu

Beat the remaining 2 cups of heavy cream until
very stiff but still spreadable. Add the crème de
cacao and mix well. Spread whipped cream
over top and sides of cake. Garnish with the
shaved milk chocolate. Cut into squares and
serve immediately.

Memories and Notes

Photos

Showered with Affection

Chapters

WEDDING SHOWER TEA

BACHELORETTE FETE

BABY SHOWER BUFFET

Wedding Shower Tea

When a woman marries, it is a time of joy, but also of transition. Her girlfriends may worry that they will be less important in the new bride's life, and she may wonder if she will still be "one of the girls." The period of preparation for the wedding is an opportune time for friends to affirm their feelings about one another. One set of girlfriends shared with us how to symbolize their connection: The friends held a tea before the wedding, and each girlfriend brought a teacup and saucer that reflected her personality and gave it to the woman about to be married. Now whenever she opens her cupboard she is reminded of the rich variety of friends who are still in her life.

Menu

SMOKED SALMON ON PUMPERNICKEL

ASPARAGUS-HAM ROLLS*

CHICKEN–CASHEW NUT SALAD*
ON SOURDOUGH BREAD

CHIVE–CREAM CHEESE AND TOMATO ON OAT BREAD

FRUIT TART*

TANGERINE CORNMEAL POUND CAKE*

SHORTBREAD COOKIES

ASSORTED TEAS

SHERRY AND PORT

ASPARAGUS-HAM ROLLS

Pencil-thin asparagus work best in this easy-to-make dish, but if all you can find are thicker asparagus, cook them about 1 minute longer (or until crisp-tender) and use 2 or 3 spears per ham slice instead of five.

Makes 16 rolls.

1 pound pencil-thin asparagus, trimmed

½ cup Dijon or honey mustard

⅔ cup finely ground plain bread crumbs

⅓ to ½ cup dry sherry

1 large bunch chives, finely chopped

1 pound thinly sliced ham (16 slices)

Bring a large pot of water to boil over high heat. Add asparagus and cook 1 minute. Remove from heat and drain well in colander. Refresh with cold water and immediately transfer to a bowl filled with ice water. When asparagus are thoroughly chilled, drain again and dry on kitchen towels.

In a medium bowl, using a fork, combine the mustard and bread crumbs. Add the sherry, starting with the smaller amount, and the chives; mix well. If the mixture is too dry, add a little more sherry or water to make it moist enough to spread.

Why do they call them showers anyway?

According to author and etiquette expert Maureen Daly, in her book *You, Too, Can Be the Perfect Hostess*: "[T]he very first shower, according to legend, was given many years ago in Holland. A little Dutch girl became engaged to a young man, who was loved by the entire village because of his many kindly, philanthropic acts. The girl's father, however, took a dim view of the marriage, since his prospective son-in-law was all-but-penniless as a result of his great generosity to friends and strangers alike. The father put his foot down on the marriage plans, so the towns-folk got together and literally 'showered' the young couple with everything needed to start the home, without parental blessing or aid. The little Dutch girl's father was so touched by the community-wide expression of love and confidence in his daughter's beau, that he finally relented and gave his fullest approval to the marriage." This, of course, sounds a bit more like legend than fact, but the shower no doubt came about as a way for more established families to help out newly married couples setting up house for the first time.

A perfect party favor

* For an inexpensive party favor, give each guest an assortment of tea bags tied together with a colorful ribbon (you may want to use ribbons that are the colors of the wedding party). Or wrap up the tea bags in squares of cloth, creating one large "tea bag" to take home.

ASPARAGUS-HAM ROLLS
(CONTINUED)

To assemble the rolls, arrange the ham slices on a flat surface. Spread each with about 1 tablespoon of the mustard–bread crumb mixture. Place 5 asparagus spears at one end of a ham slice. Roll ham tightly around asparagus to form a long tube shape. Make all the rolls in this fashion. Cut each roll in half and arrange on a platter. Serve immediately or at room temperature.

Then, too, there is the simpler tea so dear to the hearts of our hospitable ladies of good society. It was George Eliot who earnestly inquired, "Reader, have you ever drunk a cup of tea?" There is something undeniably heart-warming and conversation-making in a cup of steaming hot tea with delicious cream; it is an ideal prescription for banishing loneliness. Perhaps it is not so much the tea itself, as the circle of happy friends eager for a pleasant chat.

Lillian Eichler
*Book of Etiquette,
vol. II* (1921)

CHICKEN–CASHEW NUT SALAD ON SOURDOUGH BREAD

This method of cooking chicken produces supremely tender, thoroughly cooked meat. To prevent the cashew nuts from getting soggy, add them at the last minute as the recipe suggests.

Makes about 5 cups.

2 pounds chicken breasts (about 6 medium)

3 stalks celery, trimmed and finely chopped

½ large red onion, finely chopped

1 cup low-fat mayonnaise

¼ cup apple cider or white wine vinegar

½ teaspoon ground coriander

1¼ cups coarsely chopped toasted and salted cashews

Sliced sourdough bread

Place chicken breasts in a large pot and cover with cold water. Bring to a boil over high heat, stirring occasionally. Boil 1 minute. Remove pot from heat and cover with a tight-fitting lid. Let stand at cool room temperature 3 hours. When chicken is cool enough to handle, separate the meat from the bones, taking care to remove tendons and cartilage as well. Cut chicken into ½-inch pieces and place in a large bowl. Add the celery, onion, mayonnaise, vinegar and coriander and mix well. Season with salt and pepper. Just before serving, add the cashews and mix well. Spread on small bread squares or rounds and serve slightly chilled.

Afternoon Tea

Of course one cannot mention the words "afternoon tea" without immediately associating it with merry England. For it was there that, over two hundred years ago, a dreamy-eyed Dutchman (dreamy-eyed because he had lived many years in China) brought with him from the Orient a peculiar little leaf which, with a little hot water and sugar, made a delicious drink. At first lordly Englishmen would have none of him—but he didn't care. He exhibited the powers of the little leaves, made his tea, and drank it with relish. Others were curious; they, too, drank, and once they started it was difficult to do without it.

Someone spread the rumor that this new drink from China contained drugs and stimulants—and no sooner was this rumor spread than everyone began drinking it! Even the ladies and gentlemen of better society finally condescended to taste "the stuff"—and lo! Before they realized it, it had been unconsciously adopted as their very own beverage!

Lillian Eichler
Book of Etiquette,
vol. II (1921)

The Flower Girls

Three or four of us women had been friends with Bruce since college, and since then, he had introduced us at various parties to several couples who were also friends of his. We liked all of these people, but I wouldn't say we were particularly close, seeing each other only once or twice a year. When Bruce married for a second time, I volunteered to do the flowers for his wedding because I do that as a hobby. A couple of other friends volunteered to do the other decorations and other wedding tasks, so before we knew it, eight of us women, many of whom didn't know each other that well, were spending a lot of time together. The week before the wedding, we practically were inseparable. When the wedding was over, Bruce and Joann, his new bride, had a dinner party thanking all of us for our hard work. At one point, one of the eight women said to me, "I'm going to miss you, Gail!" and the rest of us women all chimed in that we were going to miss the easy companionship that we had found in preparing for Bruce's wedding. We decided to do something about it, so since then, we get together every two months for an event planned by one of the women. It mystifies all of us that, as a group, we have bonded so strongly and so quickly. Who knew that all of the wedding preparations would bring us so close? We eagerly anticipate our bimonthly event and, so far, we have attended a cooking class, traveled to a resort town for massages and relaxation, taken golf lessons and reenacted our party planning skills by creating a wonderful dinner for one of our group who was turning fifty. Next, a weekend in New York, and then we hope for a trip to France!

Gail

FRUIT TART

Although this recipe calls for a homemade crust, the tart is considerably easier to make than the traditional version, which calls for homemade pastry cream and fruit glaze in addition to the other components.
Makes 6 to 8 servings.

1½ cups all-purpose flour

1 tablespoon sugar

8 tablespoons unsalted butter, cut into
    pea-size pieces

1 tablespoon margarine, cut into small pieces

2 tablespoons vanilla yogurt

1 white nectarine or peach, halved and thinly
    sliced

6 ounces blackberries or other seasonal
    berries

Generously grease a 9-inch tart pan with removable bottom.

Making the dough:
In a medium bowl, combine the flour and sugar. Add the butter and margarine and using your fingers, quickly and lightly combine the ingredients until the mixture looks like rolled oats. Gently press the dough into the prepared pan, making an even bottom layer thicker than the sides. It may be necessary to occasionally wet your fingers with cold water if the dough is sticking to your hands. Refrigerate dough at least 3 hours, or up to 8 hours.

Cooking Tip

* To keep the crust crisp, assemble the fruit tart just before serving. Additionally, this delicate dessert does not hold well, so plan to serve it all in one day.

Non-cooks think it's silly to invest two hours' work in two minutes' enjoyment; but if cooking is evanescent, well, so is the ballet.

Julia Child

Thanks for everything

Diamonds and pearls are wonderful things to have on your wedding day, but nothing can replace the four precious gems—Mindy, Kim, Becky, and Fiona—that I will have standing by my side on that day. I am grateful to each one of them for coming into my life, for sharing their lives and secrets with me, for teaching me, for understanding me, for encouraging me, and most of all for loving me for me. There is no way I could even begin to describe all of the things I have been through, good and bad, with the four of them, but their presence has taught me this: Always treasure the friendships you have, and be sure to tell your friends how much you love them and how much they mean to you. Life is short, but love and true friendship are never ending.

Kimberly

FRUIT TART (CONTINUED)

Preheat oven to 425 degrees F. Place one sheet of parchment paper or foil over the bottom and sides of tart dough. Fill with pie weights or beans. Bake on bottom shelf of oven 10 minutes. Remove pie weights and parchment paper and reduce the heat to 350 degrees F. Bake 18 to 20 minutes, or until the crust is light golden brown all over. Remove from oven and cool to room temperature on a baking rack.

Assemble the tart:

When crust is completely cool, spread the yogurt over the bottom. Arrange the nectarine in a spiral design in the center of the tart. Fill the remaining space with the blackberries. Gently press the fruit into the yogurt. Slice into serving wedges and serve with a dollop of whipped cream or vanilla ice cream.

TANGERINE CORNMEAL POUND CAKE

Because this cake is not too sweet, it's good to serve for breakfast or brunch, or even as a snack with a cup of tea or coffee. This moist cake is even better the next day.
Makes about 12 servings.

Cake

1½ cups whole milk

1 cup coarse-grained cornmeal (polenta)

8 tablespoons unsalted butter, softened to room temperature

8 tablespoons margarine, softened to room temperature

1¾ cups sugar

3 eggs

½ cup tangerine juice

3 tablespoons minced tangerine zest

2½ teaspoons vanilla extract

3¼ cups all-purpose flour

1 tablespoon baking powder

1½ teaspoons baking soda

Relax!

We often find that the most stressful part of entertaining is that hour-long period immediately preceding the party, when one is racing around finishing food preparations, putting the final touches on decorations, getting dressed, and hoping frantically that no one will show up early. When planning for an event where you know that you are going to be challenged in feeling relaxed while filling your host role, consider hiring some help. It doesn't have to be expensive or elaborate. When our friend Roberta gave a shower last year, she hired another friend's twenty-year-old daughter to help out for four hours—taking coats and gifts, serving dishes, cleaning up plates. The daughter enjoyed being around this raucous group of "older" women while making a little money, and Roberta said if it was possible, she would never again throw another party without some low-cost help. While she had prepared all the food beforehand, her helper took the pressure off, and Roberta could relax while greeting and talking with her guests, the only true duties of any host!

POUND CAKE
(CONTINUED)

Serving Tip

* It is considered an honor to help serve the tea—one's closest friend is often asked to pour.

Glaze

¼ cup tangerine juice

1 cup confectioners' sugar

Scant ¼ teaspoon pure orange extract

In a medium bowl, combine the milk and cornmeal. Let stand at room temperature for at least 1½ hours, or up to 3 hours.

Preheat oven to 350 degrees F. Generously grease a fluted, 10-cup bundt pan.

In a large bowl, using an electric mixer, beat together the butter, margarine, and sugar until light in color, about 3 minutes. Add the eggs and beat about 3 minutes. Add the tangerine juice, zest, and vanilla extract and mix well. Add the flour, baking powder, and soda and mix well. Add the reserved cornmeal-milk mixture and beat 3 minutes.

Pour batter into prepared pan and bake on bottom shelf of oven 45 to 50 minutes, or until a toothpick inserted into the center of the cake comes out clean. Remove from oven and cool on baking rack. When cake is completely cool, remove from pan and place on a large plate or platter, flat side down. In a small bowl combine the tangerine juice, confectioners' sugar, and orange extract until perfectly smooth. Using a pastry brush, slowly dab the glaze over the rounded top of the cake, taking care not to dab (or pour) it on too fast, lest it all fall off the cake and onto the plate. Cut into wedges and serve.

Bachelorette Fete

Designed to give a man his "last wild night" before being married, the bachelor party was a way of acknowledging that a man was making a choice to devote his attentions to one woman only. As women have developed more independence and truly have the choice of staying single or being married, the bachelorette party has also developed as a way for girlfriends to say to their friend, "Let's celebrate your freedom one last time before you pledge yourself to the man you love." This light supper will be the perfect way to start your bachelorette party evening, whether your plans include staying in for a gabfest or venturing out for a long night of dancing and revelry.

Menu

SALMON–BELL PEPPER ASPARAGUS SOUP*

VIETNAMESE COLD NOODLE ROLLS*

TOMATOES STUFFED WITH AVOCADO-SHRIMP SALAD*

FRESH FRUIT

ASSORTED SHERBET AND FROZEN NONFAT YOGURT

SALMON–BELL PEPPER ASPARAGUS SOUP

14 cups shrimp stock (see page 60), or half and half clam juice and water

2 large Yukon Gold potatoes or white potatoes, peeled and cut into 1-inch chunks

2 large red bell peppers, stemmed and cut into 1-inch pieces

8 jumbo asparagus, trimmed and cut on the diagonal into ½-inch-long pieces

1½ pounds salmon filet, bones removed and cut into 1-inch pieces

¼ teaspoon cayenne pepper

Salt and pepper, to taste

1 bunch chives, minced

Place stock in large pot and add potatoes and bell peppers. Bring to a boil over high heat. Reduce the heat to moderate and simmer 35 to 40 minutes. Cool to room temperature. Puree in batches in a blender. Strain through a fine wire mesh (skim the foam from the surface if necessary). Transfer to a heavy-bottomed pot and bring to a boil over high heat. Reduce heat to moderate and add asparagus, salmon, and cayenne pepper. Cook 5 minutes, or until the salmon and asparagus are just cooked. Add chives, mix well, and season with salt and pepper. Serve immediately.

Dancing Feet?

* For a girlfriends party mood, or a warm-up for a night out at the hot spots, include these numbers in your music selection for the evening:

We Are Family (Sister Sledge)
Bad Girls (Donna Summer)
I Will Survive (Gloria Gaynor)
Dancing Queen (ABBA)
These Boots Are Made for Walking (Nancy Sinatra)
You've Got to Have Friends (Bette Midler)
Independent Women Part I (Destiny's Child)

Go, granny, go...

My all-time favorite bachelorette party started out as a very tame bridal shower for my high school girlfriend. We all went over to her mother's house for the shower, in this quiet little suburban neighborhood. This was when the whole Chippendale craze was really hot, so someone got the brilliant idea (without telling the rest of us) to invite a male stripper to the shower. The only problem was, all of our mothers and the bride's 80-plus-year-old, wheelchair-bound grandmother were invited as well. All of the ladies were sitting on chairs in a big circle around the room. I'll never forget the sight of this "fireman" walking into my girlfriend's living room, turning on some disco music, then ripping off his shirt and handing her a bottle of baby oil to rub on his chest. There was a startled gasp from the onlookers. The bride-to-be was beyond embarrassed, but the stripper tried to break the ice by removing his pants and then dancing suggestively around the room in a gold lamé thong. None of us knew what to do. Suddenly, the elderly grandmother, who hadn't uttered a word or even moved the entire evening, suddenly perked up, pulled out a twenty-dollar bill, motioned the stripper over, and with her frail little fingers tucked the money right into the strap of his thong. Obviously, granny knew how to handle the situation. We all roared! Evidently "the Chippendale incident," as it came to be called, got the marriage off to a good start, because my friend and her husband are still married, 25 years later.

Karen

VIETNAMESE COLD NOODLE ROLLS

Rice paper rounds come in various sizes, but look for 9-inch circles for this dish. The package contains more wrappers than called for in this recipe, but it's good to have some extra on hand when first learning how to use them and assemble the rolls. At first it may seem a little daunting, but you'll get the hang of using this wonderful ingredient after making a few rolls. Makes 8 to 10 rolls.

¼ pound skinny rice noodles

½ English cucumber, peeled and sliced into ⅛-by-5-inch-long strips

2 medium carrots, shredded

⅓ cup Thai basil leaves

⅓ cup mint leaves

½ pound cooked large prawns, peeled, tails removed, and sliced into 2 thin halves

16 to 20 9-inch rice paper rounds

In a medium pot place 4 quarts of water. Bring to a boil over high heat. Add the noodles and return to boil, stirring frequently. Boil 1 minute, remove from heat, and cover tightly for 9 to 11 minutes, or until the noodles are just tender. Strain through a fine wire mesh and transfer to a bowl.

An Easy Salad

* When assembling the stuffed tomato salad, keep it simple. We prefer just cutting up some cooked and peeled shrimp, adding 1/2-inch cubes of avocado and folding together with some lime juice. Quarter tomatoes (one for each person) from the top down, without completely cutting through the bottom of the tomatoes, and spoon the shrimp-avocado mixture inside.

Chains do not hold a marriage together. It is threads, hundreds of tiny threads, which sew people together through the years.

Simone Signoret

COLD NOODLE ROLLS
(CONTINUED)

To assemble the rolls: Place the cucumbers, carrots, basil and mint leaves, and prawns in separate bowls or piles on a flat work surface within reach. Fill a large bowl with hot water. Use two rice papers at a time and keep the remainder in the package or covered with a kitchen towel. Dip two rice paper rounds into hot water for about 20 seconds. Lift out, drain well, and place separately on a flat work surface. Let stand until wrappers are pliable, about 20 seconds. On one paper, place a few basil and mint leaves in a horizontal line about 2 inches from the bottom of the wrapper. Top with 2 to 3 slices of shrimp, about 3 tablespoons of noodles, 1 or 2 cucumber strips, and about 2 tablespoons of shredded carrot. Gently roll tightly. Place the roll at the bottom of the second (soaked) rice paper and roll tightly. If there are any small tears in the first roll, the second wrapping will remedy the problem. Make the remaining rolls in this fashion.

Memories

Include here a favorite story or photograph from a bachelorette party.

Baby Shower Buffet

Can you believe your girlfriend is a mother (or soon to be one)?
As she enters this experience, especially if it is the first time, she
is going to need all the support and encouragement she can get.
Why not marshal all her girlfriend forces at a baby shower she
will always remember?

Menu

POACHED SALMON WITH HORSERADISH–SOUR CREAM SAUCE*

CHICKEN PROSCIUTTO SPIRALS*

FRESH VEGETABLE SALAD WITH LEMON-MUSTARD DRESSING*

MEDITERRANEAN STUFFED NEW POTATOES*

ASSORTED MUFFINS AND QUICK BREADS

ASSORTED BAGELS AND YEAST BREADS

FLAVORED CREAM CHEESES AND BUTTER

ASSORTED FRESH FRUIT

SPICED PEAR CAKE WITH MAPLE FROSTING*

POACHED SALMON WITH HORSERADISH— SOUR CREAM SAUCE

If you want to double this recipe, simply purchase two salmon filets and cook separately, or together in one large sauté pan. Be sure to increase the quantity of sauce, too.
Makes about 6 servings.

1 pound salmon filet, small bones removed

2 tablespoons dry sherry

1 cup low-fat or regular sour cream

3 tablespoons horseradish

1½ teaspoons tarragon

Dash celery seed

Salt and pepper, to taste

Place salmon in sauté pan large enough to hold it in one layer. Cover with water and add sherry. Bring to a boil over high heat. Reduce the heat to moderate and simmer 7 to 9 minutes, depending the thickness of the fish. Remove from heat. Using two spatulas, lift the fish from the poaching liquid and transfer to a large plate. Cover loosely with plastic wrap and cool to room temperature, or refrigerate until chilled.

In a medium bowl, combine the sour cream, horseradish, tarragon, celery seed, salt, and pepper; mix well. To serve, cut the salmon into serving pieces and place the sauce in a small bowl next to, or in a corner of, the platter.

An Icebreaker

At a baby shower, you may have women who know the mother-to-be but have never met each other. To encourage these guests to talk to one another, give each woman a name tag printed with her name and the phrase "Ask me about...." Fill in a funny incident, a favorite passion, or recent milestone of that person's life to get the conversation rolling. Be careful with your wording, however, as Carmen found out at a recent party she hosted. Proud of her friend Cassie, who had just left a higher paying job to follow her more noble passion, Carmen included on Cassie's name tag the phrase "Ask me about my new job." Unbeknownst to Carmen, Cassie had recently had breast reduction surgery, and she thought Carmen expected her to talk about *that* job. Cassie approached Carmen, expressing her surprise at being asked to discuss her breast reduction with strangers! Aghast, Carmen explained she had wanted her to talk about her professional career. After a great laugh, Cassie rejoined the party quite content to talk about her new career, no longer feeling pressured to discuss her smaller bra size.

CHICKEN PROSCIUTTO SPIRALS

This recipe is very simple and easy to make, but it yields attractive little spirals with a zesty flavor. Serve with sweet-hot mustard, herbed vinaigrette, or a caper-mayonnaise sauce.
Makes about 8 servings.

4 boneless, skinless chicken breasts (about 2½ pounds), tendons removed

½ pound thinly sliced prosciutto

Sprigs of fresh basil or parsley, for garnish

Preheat oven to 400 degrees F. Lightly grease a 9-by-13-inch pan.

Place the chicken breasts between two pieces of plastic wrap. Using a smooth-sided meat pounder, flatten the meat to approximately ½-inch thick. Divide the prosciutto between the four chicken breasts by laying them in one layer on top of the chicken. With the long side in front of you, roll the chicken into a tight tube. You should have a long, narrow roll. Roll the remaining chicken breasts into tubes.

Place chicken rolls in prepared pan. Bake on bottom shelf of oven 20 to 25 minutes, or until the center of the chicken is cooked through. To test, remove one roll from the oven and slice in half. If the center of the chicken is opaque, remove from oven and let cool to room temperature. Wrap each roll in plastic wrap and refrigerate at least 6 hours, or up to 24 hours. To serve, slice into ½-inch-thick rounds and arrange decoratively on a large platter. Garnish with sprigs of fresh basil or parsley.

Our best wishes

* When sending out invitations, ask each guest to write down her wishes for the new baby's life. At the baby shower, each guest will read her wish and then put the slip of paper with her signature into a container, which will be sealed and presented to the mom-to-be. When the child is old enough to understand, perhaps upon reaching puberty, the new mom can open the container and share them with her son or daughter. Every child will benefit from the knowledge that all of these women are holding good wishes for him or her.

FRESH VEGETABLE SALAD WITH LEMON-MUSTARD DRESSING

I tried to select vegetables available year-round for this colorful, zesty salad. However, if you cannot find snow peas, for example, just double up on the green beans. Makes about 6 servings.

¼ cup light olive oil

2 tablespoons prepared mustard

3 tablespoons fresh lemon juice

2 tablespoons seasoned rice wine vinegar

2 large carrots, cut into ½-inch pieces

2 cups cauliflower flowerettes, ½- to ¾-inch pieces

6 ounces green beans, trimmed

10 ounces yellow pattypan squash, cut into ¾-inch pieces

8 ounces snow peas, trimmed

½ red onion, thinly sliced

Salt and pepper, to taste

In a bowl large enough to accommodate all the ingredients, combine the oil and mustard using a wire whisk to form a smooth emulsion. Slowly add the lemon juice, whisking all the while to maintain the smooth emulsion. Slowly whisk in the vinegar. Set aside until needed.

For the Worrier

* Many of us get unnecessarily stressed about entertaining and therefore entertain less than we otherwise would. If you are one of those people, put it in perspective with this passage from the book *How to Make Yourself Miserable: A Vital Training Manual.* By putting into words some of the unspoken and unreasonable worries we carry with us about entertaining (and we all do it to an extent), we can have a good laugh and see how unrealistic and destructive these concerns can be:

"If it is you who are entertaining

* Worry that nobody you invited will come, that there'll be too little food, that there'll be too much food, that they won't like the food, that nobody will mix, that they'll break your good glassware, that they'll leave cigarette burns in the upholstery, that they'll spill things on the carpet, that they'll steal something, or that they'll step on your dog or cat or child."

Of course, you can also worry about being a guest:

"If you're going to someone else's house

* Worry that you won't remember the names of people you've met before, that people you've met before won't remember your name, that nobody will talk to you, that you'll spill something or break something, or that you won't like what's being served or you'll be allergic to it and you'll either have to insult the hostess by not eating it or else eat it and be sick afterwards."

FRESH VEGETABLE SALAD (CONTINUED)

In a large pot, bring 4 quarts of water to boil over high heat. Add the carrots, cauliflower, and green beans and cook 2 minutes, stirring frequently. Add the yellow squash and cook 1 minute. Drain in a colander and refresh with cold water; drain well. Immediately add to the dressing, along with the snow peas and onion; mix well. Season with salt and pepper and serve immediately.

The ladies of America have taken the luncheon in hand and developed it into a splendid midday entertainment and means of hospitality. . . . It is usually among themselves that the ladies celebrate the ceremony of the luncheon — both formal and informal — and that it has survived, and is tending to become permanently popular, is sufficient proof of its success.

Lillian Eichler
Book of Etiquette,
vol. II (1921)

MEDITERRANEAN STUFFED NEW POTATOES

Serve these savory little bites at room temperature with a bowl of olives nearby. If you'd like to make this recipe one day ahead, be sure to tightly cover the filled potatoes with plastic wrap before refrigerating.

Makes about 8 servings.

2½ pounds small new potatoes, about 20

2 tablespoons olive oil

1 large bunch chives, finely chopped

3 tablespoons seasoned rice wine vinegar

2½ tablespoons finely chopped sun-dried tomatoes

2 tablespoons capers

Fresh parsley, for garnish

Preheat oven to 350 degrees F.

Place potatoes in large, shallow baking dish and drizzle with olive oil. Bake 25 to 35 minutes (depending on the size and freshness), or until tender when pierced with a sharp knife. Remove from oven and cool slightly. When cool enough to handle, cut 16 of the potatoes in half. Gently remove the pulp from the potato halves and transfer to a large bowl. When removing the pulp, be sure to leave a thin interior layer of potato to make them sturdy and easy to hold. Also, take care not to tear the skin.

Here come old friends...

A group of girlfriends and I celebrate the birth of a new baby by delivering a welcome home dinner. On new baby's and mom's first night home from the hospital, four girlfriends deliver a complete dinner. Each friend contributes to the dinner, which includes roast chicken, stuffing, gravy, potatoes, vegetables, salad, and dessert. All meals are prepared and ready to serve to the family when they arrive. We enlist the help of the new dad for cleanup, and we always offer to stay and baby-sit.

Cheri

...and maybe some new ones

I quit work when my first son was born, and I was afraid. I had no friends who were stay-at-home moms. I didn't know what to do with myself, and I certainly didn't know what to do with the baby. My brother suggested I volunteer at a prenatal and mothering resource center. The two other volunteers on my shift were also new mothers, our babies having been born within two months of each other. We began volunteering in the spring, and by summer were very much the Three Muskeeters (plus three). We volunteered, took the babies to the park (where my son ate sand), hung out at each other's homes, introduced our husbands, and shopped together. We horrified one salesperson, who innocently listened to our conversation about what foods disturbed the babies' digestion. Broccoli, chocolate, and very hot, spicy foods were a problem for one or more of them. After we walked away, it dawned on us that the salesperson had assumed we were feeding the babies directly with these eclectic comestibles, when we were talking about nursing them!

Martha

STUFFED NEW POTATOES
(CONTINUED)

Remove and discard the skin from the remaining 4 potatoes, and add the skinned potatoes to the pulp in the bowl. Using a fork, lightly break apart the pulp into fine pieces. Add the chives, vinegar, sun-dried tomatoes, and capers and, using a fork, lightly stir until combined. Season with salt and pepper and mix again. Mound the filling into each potato half. Arrange on a platter covered with fresh parsley leaves and serve immediately.

S P I C E D   P E A R   C A K E
W I T H   M A P L E   F R O S T I N G

This cake is so moist it really doesn't need any frosting, but the distinct flavor of pure maple and the fluffy texture of the frosting add a touch of elegance to this cake—without the added fat of traditional buttercream frosting. Makes about 8 servings.

Spiced Pear Cake

10 tablespoons unsalted butter, softened

4 tablespoons margarine, softened

1½ cups sugar

2 eggs

2 teaspoons vanilla extract

½ cup milk

2½ cups all-purpose flour

1 tablespoon baking powder

½ teaspoon baking soda

1½ teaspoons cinnamon

Dash mace and allspice

2 cups finely chopped firm pear

Preheat oven to 350 degrees F. Generously grease a 9-by-13-inch baking pan.

In a large bowl, using an electric mixer, beat together the butter and margarine. Add the sugar and mix well. Add the eggs and vanilla and mix on high speed for 3 minutes. Stir in the milk. Sprinkle over the batter the flour, baking

Baby's Here!

I like to have a "Baby's Here!" celebration shortly after my friends' babies are born. Before the birth, the expectant mom gets pampered at showers and other events, but once the baby arrives, she may feel very isolated. I've often gathered a few friends and, with them, brought over a basket of food, drinks, and pampering essentials so that the new mom doesn't feel forgotten when she's at her most exhausted and stressed. It's also helpful to go through the gifts she received and see if there are duplications or items missing, and then volunteer to make returns and exchanges. Of course, you are also there to "oooh and aaah" over the baby, but I find that the mom really needs to be the focus. Just making her a drink (nonalcoholic if she's breastfeeding, but still served in a martini or wine glass), fixing a plate of paté, cheese, and crackers, painting her fingernails, and setting up a nice foot soak with scented bath oil will remind her that she may be a mom, but she's still "one of the girls."

Veronica

Cooking Tip

* Although the maple frosting looks like it won't hold up more than a few minutes, it will keep at room temperature for several hours. It is not, however, the kind of frosting that will remain attractive and firm for more than one day.

SPICED PEAR CAKE
(CONTINUED)

powder, baking soda, cinnamon, mace, and allspice; mix until thoroughly incorporated. Mix in the pears. Pour batter into prepared pan and bake on lower shelf of oven 30 minutes. Rotate to upper shelf and bake an additional 15 to 20 minutes, or until the top is golden brown and a toothpick inserted into the center comes out clean. Cool on baking rack.

Maple Frosting

1 cup maple syrup

3 egg whites

In a small saucepan, heat the maple syrup over moderate heat until it reaches 225 degrees F. on a candy thermometer, 13 to 15 minutes. Meanwhile, in a medium bowl with high sides, beat the egg whites, using an electric mixer, until stiff. When the maple syrup reaches the proper temperature, remove from heat and cool 3 minutes. Slowly add the syrup to the egg whites in a thin stream, beating on high speed all the while to make a smooth mixture. When all the syrup has been added (this should take close to 5 minutes) beat an additional 2 to 3 minutes, or until firm enough to spread. Refrigerate until cool before frosting cake.

To frost cake, cut cake in half crosswise. Place one half on a large plate or platter. Spoon about one-third of the frosting onto the center of the cake. Gently lay the second piece on top of the frosting (the weight of the second layer will cause the frosting to even out over the first layer). Cover the top layer and sides with the remaining frosting. Serve immediately.

Memories and Notes

Photos

Enduring Traditions

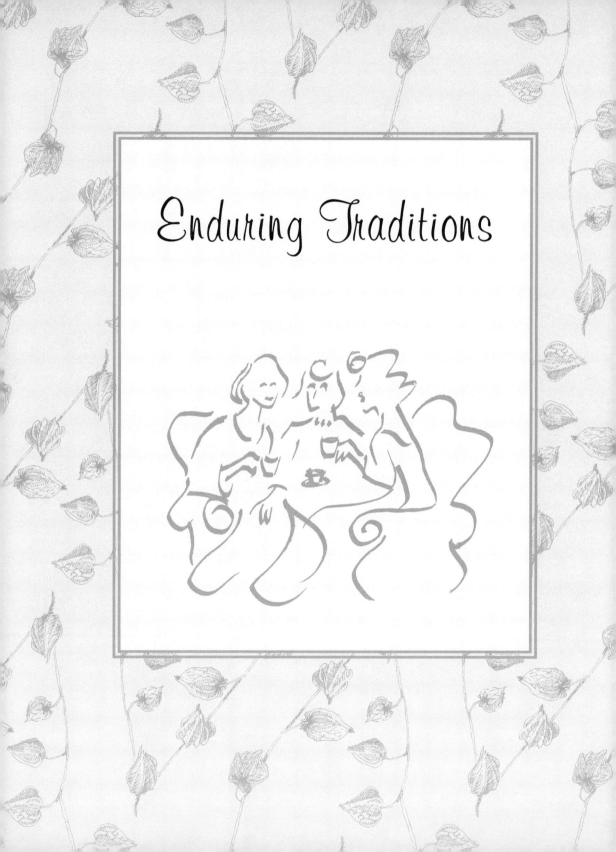

Chapters

A Sumptuous Birthday Feast

Tired of the usual cake and candles? Make this birthday celebration stand out from all the rest. With a little forethought, you can turn an ordinary birthday into an elegant event and a treasured memory shared by you and your closest friends. With this very special dinner, you will truly be expressing "I'm glad you were born."

Menu

MIXED GREENS WITH WALNUT VINAIGRETTE*

APPLE-MINT SORBET*

FILET MIGNON WITH STILTON CHEESE GLAZE*

GREEN BEANS WITH MUSHROOMS

ROASTED NEW POTATOES

BUTTER-PECAN TOFFEE ICE CREAM PIE
WITH BUTTERSCOTCH SAUCE*

SPIKED COFFEE DRINKS, ASSORTED CORDIALS,
PORTS AND/OR SCOTCH

Apple-Mint Sorbet

This refreshing sorbet will excite your taste buds with its invigorating flavor and stimulating texture.

Makes about 6 servings.

3 cups water

3 cups granulated sugar

1 cup coarsely chopped fresh mint leaves

2 large baking or tart apples, peeled, cored and finely chopped

½ cup lime juice

3 tablespoons finely chopped fresh mint leaves

Mint sprigs, for garnish

3 cups crushed ice cubes

In a 6-quart, heavy-bottomed saucepan, combine the water, sugar, and 1 cup mint leaves. Bring to a boil over high heat, stirring constantly. Boil 40 minutes or until the mixture is thick and syrupy, stirring frequently to keep the mixture from boiling over. Remove from heat and cool slightly. Strain through a fine wire mesh and return to the saucepan. Add the apples and lime juice and cook 5 or 6 minutes, or until the apples are just tender. Remove from heat and cool slightly.

In a blender, puree the mixture until smooth, stopping occasionally to scrape down the sides of the container. Transfer mixture to a plastic,

A Simple Walnut Vinaigrette

* The variety of salad dressings available in stores has greatly increased in recent years, so you will probably find a bottle of walnut vinaigrette at your local grocery store. If not, you can make it quickly yourself: Combine three parts walnut oil with one part sherry or red wine vinegar. Add salt, pepper, and a little sugar to taste and whisk together. For a more tart dressing, add a small amount of Dijon mustard to taste and whisk together. (Tip: If you have not had walnut oil before, try a bit on the tip of your finger. If the taste is too strong to you, you can substitute half of the walnut oil with olive oil.)

About Sorbet

* Sherbet and sorbet (the French word for sherbet) are thought to be the descendants of the Persian drink "charbet," comprised of sweetened fruit juice and water. Sherbet was brought from the Far East to Italy by Marco Polo in the twelfth century. Unlike sherbet, sorbet generally does not include any milk products, but often includes fruit pieces. As with this dinner, sorbet is often served as a refreshing palate cleanser.

APPLE-MINT SORBET
(CONTINUED)

glass, or stainless steel container and add the finely chopped mint leaves. Cover tightly and freeze for at least 6 hours, or up to 24 hours, stirring with a fork at least twice during this time.

To serve, place half of the crushed ice in the blender and add half of the apple mixture. Blend on high speed until the mixture is slushy. Combine the remaining ice and apple mixture and blend. Spoon sorbet into attractive glasses or small, decorative bowls and serve immediately, garnished with mint sprigs.

Gifts from the birthday girl!

If you are throwing your own shindig or just want to let your friends know what they mean to you, surprise the celebrants at your birthday party by giving them gifts! Rather than expensive items, get low-cost "symbolic" gifts—such as a small clock to represent the many years you've shared together, a decorative cord to show how strong the bond is between you, or a pair of sunglasses with the note, "You help me see the world in a better light." Take time to go around the room and say a word about each girlfriend there. It will be the birthday talked about for years to come.

FILET MIGNON WITH STILTON CHEESE GLAZE

Stilton cheese, imported from England, is an excellent cheese to use for this dish, but if it is unavailable, substitute any young, mild-tasting blue cheese like Blue Castello, Pipo Créme, Wisconsin Blue, or Gorgonzola.

Makes 6 servings.

5 ounces Stilton cheese, softened to room temperature

3½ tablespoons unsalted butter, softened to room temperature

2 cloves garlic, minced

6 6-ounce filet mignon steaks

In a small bowl combine the Stilton cheese, butter, and garlic; mix well and set aside until needed.

In a large, heavy-bottomed sauté pan, cook the steaks over moderate heat 8 to 10 minutes for medium, turning with tongs to promote even browning on both sides. Do not use a fork to turn the steaks, because puncturing the meat while it's cooking will allow all the juices to escape.

Spread some of the cheese-butter mixture on top of each steak. Reduce the heat to moderately low and cover with a tight-fitting lid. Cook about 2 minutes, or until the cheese is just starting to melt. Remove from heat and, using a spatula or tongs, transfer to plates and serve immediately.

My sixteenth birthday!

Birthdays didn't mean much to me when I was a child—at least not on a dirt-poor farm in northeastern Missouri at the end of July when there were far too many more important things to think about.

The summer before I was to graduate from high school, one of my friends decided we should learn to play softball. Since I was ready to follow Phyllis's lead in just about any of her harebrained schemes, I willingly agreed. She set a date just one week away to meet for the first practice in our local "South Park."

Unless you've experienced the hot, humid, buggy summers along the upper Mississippi River in July, you won't understand my reluctance to haul base bags, balls, bats, and water

Cooking Tip

* For wonderful roast potatoes, see page 10.

jugs out to a park. Besides, it took a long time to find a friend with a car who was free to pick up the equipment and me and drop us off at the park. Almost everyone we had asked to play that day was busy, out of town, or had some other lame excuse. Finally I found one friend who could get her father's car and take me, but she couldn't do it until the time set for practice was practically over!

It was almost 6 P.M. when we finally arrived at the softball field and started unloading all the gear. I noticed that there seemed to be a great many people in the spot we'd planned on using. Of course! I thought, I'd been so late getting there, Phyllis probably couldn't save the picnic tables and we'd just have to throw all our stuff on the ground. There didn't seem to be anyone on the playing field, however, so I assumed we'd at least be able to play.

As we were walking toward the field, our arms loaded with equipment, I noticed that one of the people sitting at the table looked very much like one of my sisters . . . and then another sister . . . my mom . . . my dad . . . my nieces and nephews . . . all my dearest friends!? What were they doing here? They had all said they were busy that day!

Then Phyllis started toward me, her smile literally spreading from ear to ear, while everyone began to sing "Happy Birthday." Not until then did I realize that it was the day of my sixteenth birthday!

There have been many birthday parties since then, but that day will be the one that lives forever in my heart. I saw Phyllis again a few years ago and felt such a rush of love and thankfulness for her. She had that very special gift of healing hearts that didn't even know they were hurting. As we embraced I felt honored beyond all else that she had seen behind my "it's just another day" façade and, with no help from anyone, showed me that I was "special."

Helen

BUTTER-PECAN TOFFEE ICE CREAM PIE WITH BUTTERSCOTCH SAUCE

If you want to reduce some of the fat and calories in this irresistible dessert, use low-fat butter pecan ice cream and nonfat, no-sugar-added vanilla ice cream. Also, low-fat graham crackers work very well in the crust.
Makes about 8 servings.

Crust

2½ cups finely crushed low-fat graham crackers

12 tablespoons unsalted butter, melted

¼ teaspoon cinnamon

Ice Cream Pie

2½ to 3 cups butter-pecan ice cream, softened slightly

7.05-ounce tin Almond Roca® or high-quality English toffee, finely chopped

2½ to 3 cups vanilla ice cream, softened slightly

My fortieth

As my fortieth birthday approached, I was asked what I wanted. I thought about it seriously and decided I wanted to be together with my girlfriends. I harmonized my heart's desire with my will, and word went out. Flight information started coming in: Liz from Lake Tahoe, Nancy from Dallas, Sylvia from Philadelphia, and Donna from Long Island. My oldest girlfriend, Gail, would be with us only in spirit as she was still immobile after a hip fracture.

We met in Queens where I lived full time and drove to our house in the country. We spent three days

Generously grease a 9-inch springform pan. Preheat oven to 350 degrees F.

In a medium bowl, use a fork to mix together the crushed graham crackers, melted butter, and cinnamon. Pour into bottom of prepared pan. Using your fingers, press the crumbs onto the bottom and 2 inches up the sides of the pan in an even layer. Bake on bottom shelf of oven 8 to 10 minutes, or until very light golden brown and aromatic. Remove from oven and cool to room temperature.

Gently spread the butter-pecan ice cream over the crust, making one even layer. Sprinkle ⅔ of the Almond Roca® over the ice cream. Place in freezer until hard. Make the second ice cream layer with the vanilla ice cream, taking care not to disturb the candy. Cover with plastic wrap and freeze 2 hours, or overnight. To serve, remove outside of pan and transfer to large plate or platter.

walking in the woods, eating wonderful food, sharing stories and photos, and listening to one another. There was a toast made to me by each of my girlfriends; a very special birthday gift from each of them.

My fortieth birthday was one of fullness. There is a picture of the five of us taken on the back deck. The golden October sky is reflected in our faces. We are glowing. When I need a lift, I look at that photo taken more than a decade ago, and it brings back all the "girlfriendness" that we still share.

Myra

ICE CREAM PIE
(CONTINUED)

Cut into serving wedges and drizzle with Butterscotch Sauce. Pass the remaining sauce.

Butterscotch Sauce

Serve this rich, creamy sauce at room temperature or slightly heated.
Makes about 2½ cups.

12 tablespoons unsalted butter

1½ cups light brown sugar

1 cup heavy whipping cream

2 teaspoons vanilla extract

In a medium, heavy-bottomed saucepan, melt the butter over moderately low heat. Add the sugar and cook 4 to 5 minutes, stirring constantly, until mixture begins to get bubbly around the edge and then over the entire surface. Remove from heat and slowly add the cream, whisking constantly. Cook over moderate heat, stirring occasionally, until the mixture begins to boil. Cook 2 minutes. Remove from heat and add vanilla extract. Cool to room temperature.

A Party Plan

- TWO WEEKS BEFORE Invite your guests.
- THREE DAYS BEFORE Plan the table decoration, figuring out what tablecloth, napkins, candleholders, candles, and flowers you will use. Can you find all of your serving pieces? Now is the time to pull them out and see if any need polishing or cleaning. If you want to set the table now, go ahead and carefully lay another tablecloth over the table to keep the dust (and the cat) from settling on the plates and silverware.
- TWO DAYS BEFORE Do your grocery shopping.
- DAY BEFORE Buy flowers and cut and put in vases on the table and around the house. Prepare apple-mint sorbet up to the final blending with remaining crushed ice and put in freezer. Make the ice cream pie and sauce.

Day of the party:

- SIX HOURS BEFORE Put any wine and/or champagne in the refrigerator. Clean the green beans, mushrooms, and potatoes and put them in the pans in which they will be cooked and into the refrigerator.
- THREE HOURS BEFORE Clean the lettuce, removing excess moisture by patting it with a paper towel, and put the cleaned lettuce, covered, in a bowl in the refrigerator so that it will remain crisp. Make the vinaigrette if you are not using bottled dressing. Put final touches, if any, on the dining table.
- ONE HOUR BEFORE GUESTS ARRIVE Make the cheese mixture for the filet mignon recipe and refrigerate. Put potatoes in the oven to roast.
- ONE-HALF HOUR BEFORE GUESTS ARRIVE Open any red or white wine you are serving to "breathe." Put on some music your guests will enjoy (after guests arrive, delegate this duty to one of them for the rest of the evening).
- IMMEDIATELY BEFORE SERVING Light the candles on the table. Pour the wine and water. Dress the lettuce and put salad bowl on table or serve onto salad plates directly. Complete the sorbet recipe by mixing the frozen apple mixture and remaining crushed ice. Put back in freezer for serving between the salad and main courses.
- BEFORE SORBET SERVING Put the steaks on to brown, turning them once during the sorbet course. Start steaming the green beans and mushrooms.
- AFTER SORBET SERVING Put steaks under the broiler with their cheese topping. Assemble steaks, potatoes, and vegetables onto plates and serve.
- AFTER MAIN COURSE Warm the butterscotch sauce for perhaps 20–30 seconds in the microwave until slightly warm. Take it out every 15 seconds or so to test warmth (you don't want to burn it—it's delicious!).

Enjoy your dessert and after-dinner drinks! Congratulations on your wonderful dinner!

What the Seasons Bring

For nineteen years, my dear friends Carrie and Suz and I have celebrated our birthdays together. We are lucky that our birthdays land in different seasons—fall, spring, and summer—so that with our busy lives we always know that we will see each other three times a year for sure. We all look forward to our nights out together to catch up on everything, solve the world's problems, and laugh ourselves sick. It is wonderful! We wish that we could see each other more during the year, but with these girlfriends it is not quantity, but quality time together that matters.

Stacy

Memories Do you have a favorite birthday memory?

Perfect Pet Party

There's only one creature who could love you better than a girl-friend—and that's your pet! Whether you're a cat, dog, ferret, or pot-bellied pig lover, you know you can count on unconditional love from your pets. Gather those girlfriends who understand this unique relationship (not all will "get it") and celebrate the birthday of your beloved furry, scaled, or feathered friend. Who deserves it more?

Menu

LOUISIANA GUMBO*

CORNBREAD

SWEET POTATO PIE*

LOUISIANA GUMBO

Any good Southern cook has a stash of bacon fat in the refrigerator—and, for that matter, chicken fat, too. However, if you're temporarily out of either, substitute vegetable oil for the bacon fat. At this point it might seem like spitting in the ocean, but for what it's worth, low-fat sausage is really an excellent product, and works very well in this deeply flavored soup. Makes about 8 servings.

5 tablespoons unsalted butter

3 tablespoons bacon fat

1¼ cups all-purpose flour

16 cups shrimp stock (see Shrimp Bisque page 60)

2 large onions, cut into dice, ¼ to ½"

2 14-ounce cans peeled and chopped tomatoes

1 teaspoon each thyme, cayenne pepper, and chili powder

½ teaspoon celery seed

Dash allspice

⅓ pound okra, trimmed and cut into ¼-inch rounds

2 green bell peppers, cut into small dice

2 stalks celery, trimmed and cut into small dice

14 ounces smoked sausage, halved and cut into ¼-inch pieces

¾ pound cooked langostino, or small shrimp

¾ pound small prawns, shells and tails removed

Salt and pepper, to taste

Cooking Tip

*   The New Food Lover's Companion tells us that a roux is a "mixture of flour and fat, that, after being slowly cooked over low heat, is used to thicken mixtures such as soups and sauces"— and particularly gumbo!

What I love about cooking is that after a hard day, there is something comforting about the fact that if you melt butter and add flour and then hot stock, it will get thick!

Nora Ephron
Heartburn (1983)

LOUISIANA GUMBO
(CONTINUED)

In a large, heavy-bottomed pot large enough to accommodate all the ingredients, melt the butter and bacon fat over moderate heat. Add the flour and cook 20 minutes, stirring frequently to prevent the roux from burning, until dark brown. Using a whisk, slowly add about 3 cups of the stock, whisking constantly to make a smooth paste. Add the stock, little by little, whisking to form a smooth mixture. When all the flour has been incorporated into the liquid, add the remaining stock, onions, tomatoes, and spices. Bring to a boil over high heat, stirring constantly with a wooden spoon, and scraping the bottom to keep the mixture from sticking and burning on the bottom. Reduce the heat to moderate and simmer 35 to 40 minutes, or until the soup is thick and the onions are tender. Add the okra, bell pepper, celery, and sausage and cook 20 minutes, or until all the vegetables are tender. Add the langostino and prawns and cook 7 to 9 minutes, or until the prawns are just cooked through. Season with salt and pepper and serve immediately.

And now for cornbread

Corn, or maize, was the staple of all early American diets, having been developed and grown by Native American Indians for more than 25,000 years before the arrival of the first European explorers. Settlers as well grew to depend on it, as it was easily portable and could be preserved through the winter months. However, as wheat growth was cultivated in the Midwest, more people in the North started turning to wheat flour; but Southerners continued to use corn for their bread products. Betty Fussell, author of *Crazy for Corn* and *The Story of Corn*, thinks this propensity may be due to the South staying more rural than the North. Now cornbread has taken on a lot of new flavors, with chefs adding many different ingredients to traditional cornbread—green chilies, cilantro, parmesan, even Bloody Mary mix (suggested by Fussell). If you are from the South, you probably have a favorite cornbread recipe in your family. If not, you can ask your favorite Southerner for his or her family recipe. Some things to remember: True cornbread has no sugar, and is best leavened with baking soda or powder instead of yeast (unlike wheat breads, which contain gluten that reacts with yeast to form the bread structure).

SWEET POTATO PIE

This popular Southern dessert is one of Janet's personal favorites, so she has tried virtually every variation, from amount and type of ingredients to the order of combining and mixing. This rendition has just the right ratio of potato to sugar, cream, and butter to make it balanced in flavor and texture—not too sweet and not so heavy—but satisfying all around. Strangely enough, though, we have made sweet potato pies with identical ingredients, and one will take 35 minutes to bake and another, 55 minutes. It must have to do with the varying water content of the potatoes. To be careful, check for doneness after about 35 minutes. Makes 6 to 8 servings.

Crust

1½ cups all-purpose flour

6 tablespoons solid vegetable shortening, such as Crisco

3 to 4 tablespoons ice water

1 egg white, for brushing dough

Filling

2 cups cooked, mashed sweet potatoes

1 cup light brown sugar

¾ cup granulated sugar

6 tablespoons unsalted butter, softened to room temperature

2 eggs

¾ cup half-and-half

2 teaspoons vanilla extract

1½ teaspoons cinnamon

Dash nutmeg

In a medium bowl, place the flour. Add the vegetable shortening in small bits. Using your fingers, lightly and quickly combine the flour with the shortening until the mixture looks like uncooked oats. Sprinkle the water over the mixture and, using your forefinger, stir until dough comes together in a ball. If it is too dry, add a little more ice water; if it is too wet, add just enough flour to make the dough come together. Press into a flat disc, wrap tightly in plastic, and refrigerate at least 4 hours, or overnight.

Preheat oven to 425 degrees F. Generously grease a 9-inch pie plate.

Lightly flour a flat surface. Roll the dough out into a 12-inch circle. Carefully lift the dough and place in the prepared pie plate. Gently press the dough into the edges of the pan and on the sides. Tuck the overhanging dough underneath itself to make a double-thick rim. Make sure the rim is resting on, not over, the flat edge of the pie plate. You will make a fluted edge by using three fingers: on one hand press your forefinger and thumb together to form a V-shape. Place these fingers on the outside of the dough rim. Using your other forefinger, press the inside of the dough into the V-shape to make a "dent." Make a fluted edge by making "dents" about ¾ of an inch apart around the edge. Lightly brush bottom and sides (but not the fluted rim) with egg white. Refrigerate the dough for at least 30 minutes, or up to 4 hours before baking.

In a large bowl, using an electric mixer, beat together the sweet potatoes and sugars until well mixed. Add the butter and beat 1 minute. Add the eggs, half-and-half, vanilla, and spices and beat 2 minutes. (The mixture may not have a smooth appearance.) Pour the mixture into the prepared crust. Bake on bottom shelf of oven for 15 minutes. Reduce the heat to 350 degrees F. and bake 55 to 60 minutes, or until the center barely jiggles when shaken. Remove from oven and cool to room temperature on baking rack. Will keep at a cool room temperature for up to 2 days covered with plastic wrap.

DOG BIRTHDAY CAKE

The cakes Janet made for Domino were usually three layers high and "frosted" with some relatively smooth canned food thinned with a little water. The outside of each one was decorated with a different type of doggie treat—small, multicolored bones for the bottom layer; imitation bone slices for the second layer, and maybe liver treats on the smallest, top layer. Beef jerky sticks made perfect candles and stayed in place while carrying the cake outside.

Make the base of the cake with overcooked (sticky) rice mixed with a little cooked and defatted ground beef, minced cooked lamb, or chicken, depending on the dietary needs and gustatory desires of your pooch. If you're pressed for time, use semichunky canned food to mix with the rice instead. You'll need to refrigerate this mixture just long enough to make it easy to handle. Remember, all three layers are made with this rice-meat combo, so it has to be firm enough to hold a shape and sustain the weight of one or two additional layers.

Once all three layers are in place, mix the "frosting" and apply. Decorate as you wish and count out the beef jerky candles. Do not refrigerate the cake or serve it cold, as dogs need to eat their food at room temperature (or warm).

Pet Party Favors

* Animal lovers are special people. They realize that pets are people with hair (or scales or feathers or…). Since this is one of the few times bringing your pet to a party is socially appropriate, make the most of it. If all the pets wear collars, have an inexpensive dog or cat tag made with the event and the date of the event written on it. As the host, or attendee, bring a paper party hat for each pet. If they won't wear the hats, then insist that their humans do.

Domino

Every year I made a special cake for Domino, my wondrous Great Dane. Since he didn't want to eat human food (and since I'd never feed it to him anyway), his cakes were composed of various commercial dog foods and treats, plus cooked rice and beef or lamb.

I used a huge plastic tray for Domino's cake, since he wasn't the only one indulging. On that note, be sure to invite polite dog friends to share in the festivities. I say polite because, generally speaking, if you put a dog cake made with the aforementioned delicacies before several canines at once, chances are fur will stiffen and tempers flare. Of course, my precious pooch had the manners of nobility and the grace of an angel, really—he was referred to as a prince in a Great Dane suit. So at our house, birthday celebrations always included his girlfriends, Mattie and Baily, and once in a while a fellow (neutered) boy-buddy.

Another word of caution: Your canine companion may have a stomach of steel, but in case he or she is sensitive, be prudent about the quantity of treats used for decoration. This is a celebration for your dog, but as I used to tell Domino, "I'm the one with the opposing thumbs and checkbook—that means I get to make the important decisions around here." I'm sure his response was, "Yeah, right Mom, whatever you say," as he dialed up his financial advisor and poured himself a glass of scotch.

Janet

Pet Party Pics
Cut out some pictures of your favorite pet event and place here.

Holiday Cookie Classic

Our friend Nenelle has a wonderful way to celebrate the holiday season: She sets a time, usually a Saturday afternoon in early December, to invite all of her girlfriends to her home. Supplying drinks and snacks, she asks all of her friends to bring one type of cookie dough, which they have already prepared but not baked. (If you wish, you can pass out the recipes included here, one to a person, and ask that they bring the prepared dough.) As all of the cookies brown in her oven, filling the house with wonderful holiday smells, the girlfriends have time to catch up with each other.

And each will go home with a tin of assorted cookies! You may also ask them to bring all of their holiday catalogs. As the cookies bake, each woman can get some holiday shopping done (as well as get some ideas of what their friends would like as gifts), all without fighting traffic or leaving the house!

Menu

CHECKERBOARD COOKIES*

ORANGE SHORTBREAD*

CREAM WAFERS*

COCONUT-DATE-WALNUT BALLS*

WALNUT-CINNAMON RUGULA*

TOFFEE CHIP COOKIES*

GINGERBREAD PEOPLE

VEGETABLE CRUDITE PLATTER

FRESH FRUIT

EGGNOG, SPIKED APPLE-GINGER CIDER,* HOT CINNAMON SHOTS,
SPICED FRUIT TEA,* bottled water and soft drinks

CHECKERBOARD COOKIES

When testing this recipe, Janet's darling "neighbor girls" were visiting, so we asked them to help by writing down the directions step by step as she assembled the dough into the checkerboard pattern. Thanks to their excellent listening and writing skills, the recipe has clear directions to aid in making these stunning cookies.

Makes about 40 cookies.

10 tablespoons unsalted butter, softened to room temperature

8 tablespoons margarine, softened to room temperature

1¾ cups sugar

1½ tablespoons vanilla extract

3 cups all-purpose flour

½ cup cocoa

To make the basic dough: In a large bowl, using an electric mixer, beat together the butter, margarine and sugar 1½ minutes on high speed. Add 1 tablespoon of the vanilla and mix well. Place one-half of the mixture in a separate bowl. For the vanilla dough, add the remaining vanilla extract and 1¾ cups flour; beat on medium speed until the mixture starts to clump together, about 30 seconds. Do not overmix. Remove the dough and form into a rectangle approximately 10 inches long and 2 inches wide.

Cooking Tip

* Butter and margarine produce different textures in baked goods: A cookie made with all butter will flatten out more while baking and take on a richer flavor and somewhat oily texture. Margarine can effect a more crumbly, firm texture, but it lacks the delicious flavor of sweet butter. Therefore, the combination of both fats provides a wonderful balance of flavor, appearance, and texture in baked goods.

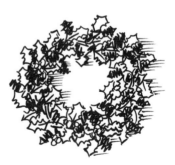

CHECKERBOARD COOKIES
(CONTINUED)

To make the chocolate dough, add the remaining flour (1¼ cups) and the cocoa. Mix on medium speed until the mixture starts to clump together. Do not overmix. Remove the dough and form into a rectangle approximately 10 inches long and 2 inches wide.

Place the vanilla dough rectangle on top of the chocolate dough rectangle and press gently to adhere. Cut through both doughs lengthwise through the center, making two 10-by-1-inch rectangles. Take one section and lay it on its side. Take the other section and place it on top so that the chocolate is on top of the vanilla and the vanilla is on top of the chocolate. Using the top of the dough as the guide, cut the vanilla side down the center lengthwise, and the chocolate side down the center lengthwise. You now have one thick section in the center and two skinny outside pieces. Lay one of the skinny sections down and top with the thick piece, once again placing the vanilla on top of the chocolate and the chocolate on top of the vanilla. Place the remaining skinny piece on top, alternating flavors. Wrap the dough tightly in plastic wrap and gently wrap on flat surface to even out and straighten the sides of the block. Refrigerate for 8 hours, or overnight.

Preheat oven to 350 degrees F. Grease two cookie sheets and cover with parchment paper. Using a sharp knife, cut dough into ¼-inch-thick slices. Place on cookie sheets approximately 2 inches apart. Bake one sheet at a time on upper shelf 12 or 13 minutes, or until edges are slightly golden brown. Bake remaining cookies in this fashion.

CREAM WAFERS

It's nice to have a cookie delicate in flavor and texture when serving such a variety of rich and fancy confections.

Makes about 18 cookies.

8 tablespoons unsalted butter, softened to room temperature

4 tablespoons margarine, softened to room temperature

1½ cups sugar

1 tablespoon vanilla extract

⅓ cup heavy cream

2 cups all-purpose flour

In a large bowl, using an electric mixer, beat together the butter, margarine and ½ cup of the sugar 3 minutes on high speed. Add the vanilla extract and cream and beat well (the mixture may look curdled). Add the flour and beat just until incorporated, about 30 seconds or less. Cover dough and refrigerate at least 4 hours, or overnight.

What to have on hand for your cookie party

(besides the cookie dough, of course):

* Lots of cookie sheets
* Butter for greasing pans
* Parchment paper (available at the grocery store, it helps keep cookies from getting too brown on the bottom)
* Cookie tins so everyone can take home a selection of cookies
* Notepads and pencils so everyone can write down gift ideas, recipes, and catalog phone numbers or websites
* Holiday music

Preheat oven to 350 degrees F. Grease two cookie sheets and cover with parchment paper. Roll dough into balls about the size of a large walnut (in the shell). Roll in sugar and place on cookie sheets about 3 inches apart. Dip a flat-bottomed glass into sugar and flatten dough to between ⅛ and ¼-inch thick. Bake one sheet at a time on upper shelf 18 to 20 minutes, or until bottoms and edges are golden brown. Remove from oven and gently transfer to baking rack using a spatula. Bake remaining cookies in this fashion.

ORANGE SHORTBREAD

These buttery, crumbly treats are hard to resist—you might want to double the recipe. Be sure to use high-quality butter when making shortbread.
Makes 16 pieces.

16 tablespoons unsalted butter, softened to room temperature

¾ cup sugar

2 teaspoons vanilla extract

1½ tablespoons minced orange zest

2½ cups all-purpose flour

6 tablespoons cornstarch

Preheat oven to 325 degrees F. Generously grease an 11-inch glass pie pan.

In a medium bowl, using an electric mixer, beat together the butter and ½ cup of the sugar on high speed 2 minutes. Add the vanilla and orange zest and mix well. Add the flour and cornstarch and mix 1 minute on high speed to thoroughly combine. Gather dough into a ball and transfer to the prepared pie plate. Using your fingers, gently press the dough onto only the bottom of the pie pan—not up the sides—in one even layer. Using a sharp knife, cut into 16 triangles. Pierce dough all over using the tines of a fork.

Bake on lower rack of oven 45 minutes. Rotate to upper shelf and bake additional 10 to 15 minutes, or until top is light golden brown. Remove from oven and, using a sharp knife, re-cut along the lines to facilitate breaking the cookies apart once cooled. Sprinkle with remaining sugar. Cool on a baking rack. Shortbread will keep at room temperature tightly covered with plastic wrap, or in a tightly sealed plastic bag, for up to 4 days.

COCONUT-DATE-WALNUT BALLS

You won't believe how easy and fast these cookies are to make—and so scrumptious and satisfying. To facilitate chopping the dates, place them in the freezer for 30 to 45 minutes, or until hard but not frozen. Chop in a food processor, or by hand with a large, very sharp chef's knife. Makes about 30 cookies.

2 cups finely chopped pitted dates

2 cups finely chopped walnuts

2 cups shredded coconut

1 14-ounce can nonfat sweetened condensed milk

1½ teaspoons cinnamon

Dash mace

In a medium bowl, combine all the ingredients until thoroughly mixed. Cover and refrigerate until chilled, at least 2 hours or up to 8 hours.

Preheat oven to 350 degrees F. Grease two cookie sheets and cover with parchment paper. Using about 1½ tablespoons of dough per cookie, shape mixture into balls and place approximately 2 inches apart on cookie sheets. Flatten slightly with your hand. Bake one sheet at a time on upper shelf 15 to 17 minutes, or until very lightly browned around the edges. Remove from oven and let cool 1 minute before transferring to baking rack to cool. Bake remaining cookies in this fashion.

Homemade Surprises

For years, Susie and I found time to create homemade surprises for one another and for our growing families. Our respective talents yielded personalized needlepoint pieces, salt dough figures documenting activities of the past twelve months, crocheted afghans, gardening time-savers, jams made from summer-harvested berries, hand-painted tiles, and anything else with which we were currently experimenting. At Christmastime, it became a tradition to save our special boxes as the "grand finales" of our gift-opening sessions.

Ellen

Guidelines for a successful girlfriend event

* SHARE THE SPOTLIGHT

Don't focus on one person or one topic for the entire event; be considerate if there is a minority of single, pregnant or married women—be inclusive!

* LET'S TALK ABOUT CHILDREN

If you have children, don't ask to bring them to the party. It puts the host on the spot—if she allows yours, she has to allow everyone's children to come, and she may not have the space or facilities. While children are often specifically included in parties and invitations, they do change the social dynamic. So when necessary, get a sitter for the kids and give your girlfriends your full attention. If you're the host, and you only want grown-ups at your event, simply indicate "grown-ups only" or a similar phrase on your invitation.

* LET'S TALK ABOUT PETS

If you have the impulse to bring your pet to a girlfriends gathering, please read the above and substitute the word "pets" wherever you read "children," except you probably don't need a sitter for your pet! The exception to this rule is when you're attending a pet birthday party and the host is expecting you and your little friend.

* SHOW COURTESY

RSVP promptly to invitations requesting a response. If you have responded yes, don't cancel at the last minute or fail to show up without a very good reason.

* GET YOUR PRIORITIES STRAIGHT

Never show disrespect for your girlfriends by canceling a date with them for a date with a man or anyone else. You risk offending the women who love you most and can appear desperate to the man who asked you out. If he's a keeper, he'll ask again. Better yet, ask him.

* MODIFY YOUR MENU ACCORDINGLY

In this day and age, everyone seems to have specific dietary requirements. Don't fight it. Your event will go more smoothly if you take into account the person on a diet, the vegetarians, the vegans, the individuals restricted from wheat products, and others with special dietary needs.

WALNUT-CINNAMON RUGULA

This marvelous Jewish confection is also made with miniature chocolate chips, but we prefer the more subtle version presented here, made with walnuts and cinnamon.

Makes about 48 cookies.

2½ cups all-purpose flour

½ cup sugar

12 tablespoons chilled, unsalted butter, cut into pea-size pieces

8 ounces cream cheese, pulled apart into small bits

2 cups very finely chopped walnuts

1¼ cups sugar

2 tablespoons cinnamon

I feel a recipe is only a theme, which an intelligent cook can play each time with a variation.

Madame Benoit
Canadian cooking expert

In a large bowl, mix together the flour and sugar. Add the butter and cream cheese and, using your fingers, quickly mix together, incorporating the fat into the dry ingredients, until the mixture resembles rolled oats. Gather dough together and form into a 9-inch log. Cut log in thirds and form each into a disc. Wrap tightly in plastic and refrigerate 8 hours, or overnight.

In a medium bowl, combine the walnuts, sugar, and cinnamon.

Preheat oven to 350 degrees F. Grease two cookie sheets and cover with parchment paper. Working with one disc at a time, sprinkle some of the walnut-sugar mixture on a flat surface. Using a rolling pin, roll dough into a circle approximately 13 inches in diameter. To keep the dough from sticking, be sure to use enough sugar mixture under and on top of the dough as you roll it. Using a sharp knife, cut the circle like a pizza into 16 triangles. Sprinkle more sugar mixture over the dough. Using one triangle at a time, roll up from the wide end to the point. Roll the remaining triangles in this fashion. Place on cookie sheets approximately 2 inches apart. Bake one sheet at a time on the upper shelf 18 to 20 minutes, or until light golden brown and aromatic. Remove from oven and transfer to baking rack to cool. Prepare and bake remaining cookies in the same fashion.

A Time for Everyone

My favorite tree trimming party involves inviting several of my girl-friends, along with their children, to my home. Before the guests arrive, I put the tree up and string the lights on it, leaving large baskets filled with decorations around the room. Several "children's baskets" contain only cloth ornaments with bows (no metal hooks). Many of my guests arrive with their own homemade ornaments to add to the collection. I provide drinks, snacks, desserts, music, and activities for the children, who range from teenagers to toddlers. The teenagers make great baby-sitters, and the grown-ups are left free to enjoy themselves.

The only rule is that everyone has to put at least one ornament on the tree before they leave. Some years, the tree is decorated before I know it. Other years, the night has been almost over with the tree still looking empty, and everyone scrambles around to fin-ish the tree before they say goodnight. Whatever the case, everyone enjoys the laughs, the friendship, and the holiday cheer; and I end up with a decorated tree!

Cheri

SPIKED APPLE-GINGER CIDER

This aromatic elixir is very refreshing made without alcohol and served chilled. For cold weather entertaining, spike it with vodka and present it piping hot ladled into decorative mugs.

Makes about 2 quarts.

1.5 liters apple cider or apple juice

1 25.4-ounce bottle plum wine or sweet white wine

⅓ cup sugar

1 8-inch piece fresh gingerroot, peeled and cut into ½-inch pieces

1 vanilla pod, split lengthwise

½ cup vodka or other liquor, to taste

In a large, heavy-bottomed pot combine the apple cider, plum wine, sugar, and gingerroot. Using a sharp knife, gently scrape the seeds from the inside of the vanilla pod into the liq-uids. Bring to a boil over high heat. Reduce the heat to moderate and simmer 30 minutes, stir-ring occasionally. Remove from heat and cover with a tight-fitting lid. Let stand at room tem-perature until cool. Strain through a fine wire mesh. Add vodka and mix well. Serve chilled or warm.

Toffee Chip Cookies

Everyone likes chocolate chip cookies, but we have found these sumptuous toffee chip cookies to be just as popular.
Makes 22 to 24 cookies.

12 tablespoons unsalted butter, softened to
    room temperature

¾ cup sugar

¾ cup light brown sugar

2 eggs

2½ teaspoons vanilla extract

2½ cups all-purpose flour

¾ cup old-fashioned oatmeal

¼ teaspoon baking soda

1 10-ounce bag toffee chips (or 1¾ cups finely
    chopped English toffee)

Cooking Tip

* If your grocery store doesn't stock toffee chips (found in the baking section along with the other "chips"), substitute any high-quality toffee without a chocolate coating. If you cannot find plain toffee, you can use broken-up pieces of Almond Roca®, or Heath® or Skor® bars instead. You will just have to tolerate a bit of chocolate in your cookies as well—too bad!

In a large bowl, using an electric mixer, beat together the butter and sugars 1 minute on high speed. Add the eggs and vanilla extract and beat 1½ minutes. Add the flour, oatmeal, and baking soda and mix well. Stir in the toffee chips. Cover and refrigerate dough until thoroughly chilled, about 1½ hours.

Preheat oven to 350 degrees F. Grease two cookie sheets and cover with parchment paper. Using about 1½ rounded tablespoons per cookie, shape the dough into balls and place on cookie sheets approximately 2½ inches apart. Pat down the top of the balls slightly. Bake one sheet at a time on the upper shelf 15 to 17 minutes, or until the tops are golden brown, rotating the sheet halfway through to promote even browning. Remove from oven and let cool 1 minute before removing from cookie sheet with a spatula and placing onto a baking rack. Bake remaining cookies in this fashion.

SPICED FRUIT TEA

You may want to purchase the ingredients for this comforting brew in a natural food store where cinnamon sticks and dried pears are sold in bulk, and cinnamon-apple spice tea and dried orange peel are standard commodities. Makes about 3½ quarts.

4½ quarts (18 cups) water

12 cinnamon-apple spice tea bags

4 cinnamon sticks

7 ounces dried pears, halved

3 tablespoons dried orange peel

Honey, to taste

Place all ingredients except the honey in a large, heavy-bottomed pot. Bring to a boil over high heat. Reduce the heat to moderate, cover, and simmer 20 minutes. Remove from heat and let stand at room temperature, covered, until cool. Strain through a fine wire mesh. Add honey to taste. Serve chilled or warm.

Don't worry, it happens to everyone

With everything you've got to think about when hosting a girlfriends event, don't add "worry about my messy kitchen" to your list. Don't bother trying to keep your guests out of it either. Everyone is going to end up in the kitchen at one point or another, and every woman who attends has had a messy kitchen, so take a deep breath and let the kitchen be, no matter what shape it is in when guests arrive. Or go ahead and make your kitchen the center of activity:

* Add some candles and flowers to create a warm atmosphere as you finish your preparations.

* If you like an organized kitchen while preparing food (and want to put your friends to work), create "stations" where one person is asked to serve drinks, one is chopping vegetables, one is folding napkins, etc.

Memories and Notes

Photos

Endnotes

Women in the Wild

Amy Vanderbilt, *Amy Vanderbilt's Everyday Etiquette* (New York: Bantam Books, 1956), 21-22.

Corn on the Cob: See in Chapter XXXV, "The Kindergarten of Etiquette" by Emily Post, *Etiquette* (New York: Funk & Wagnalls, 1922) at http://www.bartleby.com/95/35.html.

Friday Night Film Fest

Maureen Daly, *You, Too, Can Be The Perfect Hostess* (New York: Pocket Books, Inc., 1950), 66.

Nachos: See Cheryl Alters Jamison and Bill Jamison, *The Border Cookbook: Authentic Home Cooking of the American Southwest and Northern Mexico* (Boston: Harvard Common Press, 1995), quoted in www.lardbiscuit.com/lard/nachos.htm, D. Trull, Nachos Rule! The Secret Origin of the #1 Greatest "Mexican" Food, *The Lard Letter*, January 1996.

Nachos: See Nachos, anyone? by Adriana P. Orr in *Oxford English Dictionary News* (July 1999) at www.oed.com/public/news/9907_2.htm#nachos.

Jicama: See *Merriam-Webster's Collegiate Dictionary, 10th Edition* (Springfield, MA: Merriam-Webster Inc., 1993), 629.

Just Talk

Diane Ackerman, *A Natural History of the Senses* (New York: Vintage Books, 1990), 130.

A Housewarming Dinner

What are the differences among kosher salt, sea salt and table salt?
See Anne Garber, "All About Salt," 2001 at http:www2.alberta.com/food/columns/display-one.efm?articleid=242.

Housewarming: See Julienne Bennett and Mimi Luebberman, ed., *Where the Heart Is: A Celebration of Home* (Novato, CA: New World Library, 1994), 160-161. By permission of Holly Rose.

Hallelujah Lunch

Vanilla: See Diane Ackerman, *A Natural History of the Senses* (New York: Vintage Books, 1990), 158-160.

Wedding Shower Tea

Why do they call them showers anyway?
Maureen Daly, *You, Too, Can Be The Perfect Hostess* (New York: Pocket Books, Inc., 1950), 181.

Tea: See in Chapter IV, "Teas and other Entertainments," by Lillian Eichler, *Book of Etiquette, vol. II* (Oyster Bay, N.Y.: Nelson Doubleday, Inc., 1921)

Baby Shower Buffet

Worrier: See Dan Greenberg with Marcia Jacobs, *How to Make Yourself Miserable: A vital training manual* (New York: Random House, 1966), 25.

A Sumptuous Birthday Feast

Sorbet: See Beating the Heat with Frozen Treats at
http://www.creativeseasoning.com/Recipes/FrozenTreats.htm.

Perfect Pet Party

Roux: See Sharon Tyler Herbst at http://www.allrecipes.com/encyc/terms/R/8286.asp (excerpted from *The New Food Lover's Companion, second edition* (Barron's Educational Series, 1995).

Cornbread: See Chef's Corner, Jon Bullard (8/19/1998) at
http://www.newsherald.com/archive/food/cc081998.htm.

Cornbread: See quote by Betty Fussell in Christine Arpe Gang, "Heavenly cornbread"
(3/25/1998) at www.s-t.com/daily/03-98/03-25-98/c01ho114.htm.

Index

About the Press

Wildcat Canyon Press publishes books that embrace such subjects as friendship, spirituality, women's issues, and home and family, all with a focus on self-help and personal growth. Great care is taken to create books that inspire reflection and improve the quality of our lives. Our books invite sharing and are frequently given as gifts.

For a catalog of our publications, please write:

Wildcat Canyon Press
2716 Ninth Street
Berkeley, California 94710
Phone: (510) 848-3600
Fax: (510) 848-1326
Visit our website at www.wildcatcanyon.com